DISCOVER YOUR SPLENDOR
in Your Life

Unleash
the Power
of Authentic
Purpose and
Mission

Also by Splendor Publishing

La Musica
Are You Playing Your Song?

Positive x Positive = Unlimited
High Octane Positive Energy

The Art & Science of Loving Yourself First
'cause Your Business Should Complete You Not Deplete You

25 Brilliant Business Mentors
Their Top Tips to Catapult You to Success

25 Brilliant Speakers
Their Expert Advice to Springboard Your Speaking Career

The Happy Law Practice
Expert Strategies to Build Business While Maintaining Peace of Mind

Winning Ways in Commercial Real Estate
18 Successful Women Unveil the Tips of the Trade in the Real Estate World

The Substance of Faith
Get Hooked—It's Good Stuff

DISCOVER YOUR SPLENDOR
in Your Life

Unleash the Power of Authentic Purpose and Mission

Splendor Publishing
College Station, TX

SPLENDOR PUBLISHING
Published by Splendor Publishing,
College Station, TX.

Copyright © Margo DeGange, M.Ed., Splendor Publishing, 2016.
All Rights Reserved Worldwide

No part of this book may be used, reproduced, uploaded, stored, or introduced into a retrieval system, or transmitted in any way or by any means (including electronic, mechanical, recording, or otherwise), without the prior written permission of the publisher, with the exception of brief quotations for written reviews or articles. No copying, uploading, or distribution of this book via the Internet is permissible.

The authors and publisher have made every effort to include accurate information and website addresses in this work at the time of publication, and assume no responsibility for changes, omissions, inaccuracies, or errors that occur before or after publication. The publisher does not endorse or assume responsibility for information, author or third-party websites, or their content.

Library of Congress Control Number: 2016902745
Discover Your Splendor in Your Life:
Unleash the Power of Authentic Purpose and Mission

ISBN-10: 1-940278-14-7
ISBN-13: 978-1-940278-14-8
1. Self Help 2. Spirituality

Printed in the United States of America.

Cover art: © Mark J. Grenier, 34526440 | Dreamstime
Interior photos and illustrations, Dreamstime:
Introduction, © Kirsty Pargeter, 92968; Ch. 1, © Delmas Lehman, 21284855; Ch. 2, © Alphaspirit, 22460778; Ch. 3, © Andrejg5, 29951214; Ch. 4, © Johanna Goodyear, 183888; Ch. 5, © Abdone, 145411; Ch. 6, © Anatoly Tiplyashin, 214975; Ch. 7, © Solarseven, 31707174; © Mark J. Grenier, 34526440 | Dreamstime

For more information or to order bulk copies of this book for events, seminars, conferences, or training, contact SplendorPublishing.com.

Dedication

This book is dedicated to you, the inquisitive reader, who
desires to find that space in life where you know you are
contributing, using your gifts, tapping into passion,
creating new and positive outcomes, being
creative, experiencing joy, and making
a difference for others. We have
enormous love and respect for
your decision to do so,
and we are greatly
honored to share
this journey
with you.

"We all come into this world with our own special gifts, our own unique colorful hues, our own vibrant touch, and our own beautiful harmony waiting to be shared with others."

Giovanni Gaudelli

Contents

FOREWORD — XIII
Giovanni Gaudelli

INTRODUCTION: *We Want More* — 1
Margo DeGange

CHAPTER 1: *If Not a Moose Then a Goose* — 9
Timothy Grant Carter

CHAPTER 2: *Your "Gift of Brilliance"* — 25
Margo DeGange

CHAPTER 3: *This is Your Decade* — 45
Dorothy-Inez Del Tufo

CHAPTER 4: *From Here to There-A Birthday Epiphany* — 55
Virginia Kettler

CHAPTER 5: *Authentic Purpose* — 67
Anthony McCauley

CHAPTER 6: *It's Okay* — 81
Heather McKim

CHAPTER 7: *Laughing at the Future* — 91
Karen V. Smith

CHAPTER 8: *Do What You Must* — 109
Timothy Grant Carter

Foreword

The rest of your life begins today. What do you want it to look like? What do you want to do with it? How do you want to feel? Sooner or later you will be asking yourself these questions. How about starting right now?

We live in an era where the average life expectancy hasn't been higher. So *how* we live becomes more important than ever; and even more important than how, is *why*. Sadly, we tend to let all the demands, hustle, and bustle of life get in the way, creating a disconnection between our *how* and our *why*.

The greatest lesson I have learned on my life's journey is that we're all naturally creative, resourceful, and whole. We all come into this world with our own special gifts, our own unique colorful hues, our own vibrant touch, and our own beautiful harmony waiting to be shared with others. I refer to this as our internal "musica." It is so strong that when you look into a baby's eyes, you can literally feel it.

Finding or reconnecting with our purpose—our "why"—is the key that opens the door to all our resources and gifts. It makes us want to get up in the morning with a smile on our face and a spring in our step, no matter what our "job" is. It determines whether we're just "filling up" time or experiencing deep fulfillment. It keeps us going even if the odds seem to be against us. It keeps us whole, healthy, and dynamic whether we are just starting out in life or heading toward retirement. It makes us feel like our contribution matters because we are driven by a cause that is close to our heart. Our actions reach and touch others in more ways than we can imagine, and that in itself is one of the most rewarding senses of fulfillment that we can ever feel.

So, how do we find or rekindle our purpose?

Sometimes, all we need is for someone to help us find the key so we can unlock the door to all those amazing gifts that we carry within us. This is what the coauthors of this magnificent book, *Discover Your Splendor in Your Life: Unleash the Power of Authentic Purpose and Mission*, can do for you. They will help you embrace a life that's an expression of your true values. Their personal experiences and stories will move and inspire you. Their strategies will give you the courage to spread your wings and honor your calling.

This book is a wonderful opportunity for you to start creating a more fulfilling life with a deeper sense of meaning and a level of satisfaction that will create a beautiful harmony within and around you.

May the rest of your life be "magnifico"!

Giovanni Gaudelli
Best-selling Author of *La Musica—Are You Playing Your Song*,
International Motivational Speaker, and
Certified Professional Coach,
Montreal, Quebec, Canada.
Website: *GioMotivation.com*

Introduction

It Matters

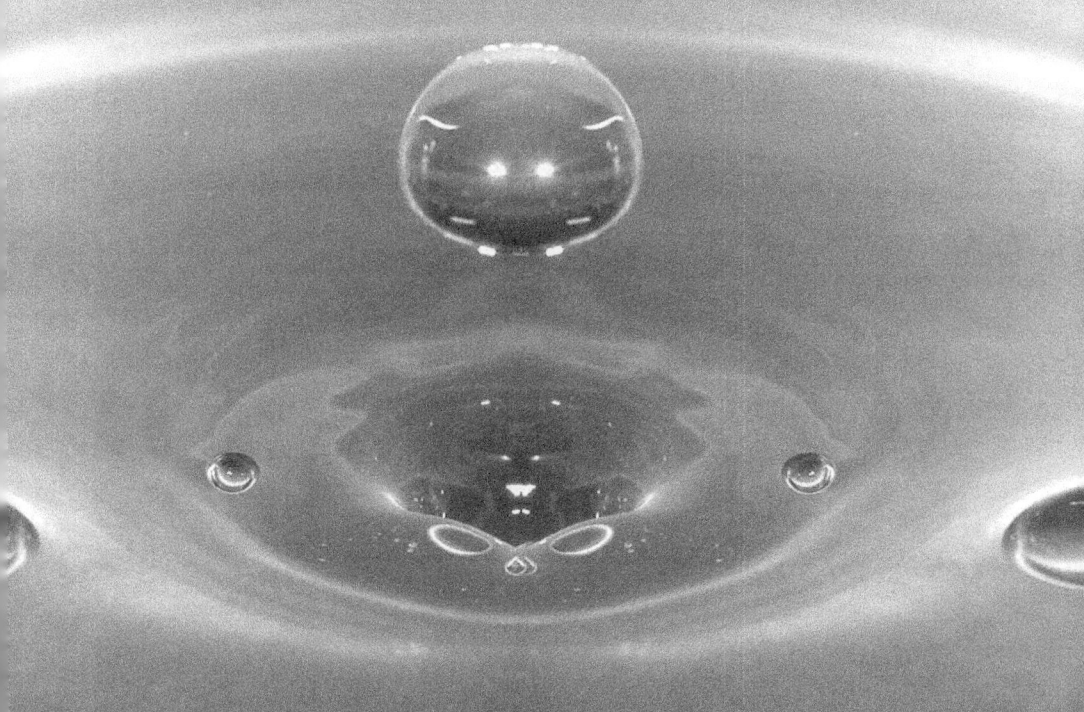

"There are few things more powerful than a life lived with passionate clarity."

Erwin Raphael McManus

We Want More

What has happened to the likes of us? We live in a world where on all sides we are bombarded with activity and technology, and we are constantly faced with increasing distraction: people, play things, and projects that cry out for way too much of our time and attention. Then of course there are the "other" people, play things, and projects that don't get enough.

We're a Little Numb

We move fast! Typically, we don't slow down long enough or give ourselves enough reflection time to consider the "view" or the "environment" of our day-to-day life, or to fully understand the impact our decisions and actions (or lack thereof) have on ourselves and others. We talk and interact incessantly, but in reality we say and communicate very little.

We may question whether or not we are focusing on the "right" things or the "important" people. With our limited time frames, limitless diversions, and ever demanding schedules, we may wonder if we are choosing wisely . . . or even if we are being smart about which choices we want on the table in the first place.

What's more, in our continual movement and bustle, we don't give ourselves permission—or create any kind of a process—to pull the brakes or completely change course, even if it were truly needed or desired. Then, to avoid the pain of such truth, we may actually pretend it's all perfectly *as it should be*, which in turn gives us no reason to change a thing. We sort of go numb—at least a bit.

Then There Are Those "Awakened" Ones

At the same time (as crazy as it seems), there is a great deal of talk today—from those who are at least a little more enlightened—about *making a difference, knowing your purpose, finding your calling, discovering your strengths,* and *uncovering your passion* (that "thing" about which you are most "on fire"). We are highly encouraged to *leave a legacy, know our life's mission, serve the less fortunate,* and *lead our tribe,* because, we are told, it is *bigger than just us,* and *not all about us*!

These popular buzz-words and phrases may be considered cliché, yet when we hear them they trigger something deep within, that causes us to wonder if our lives are significant and meaningful enough. That in turn causes us to either reflect as best we can, or wish we had the time and luxury to do so.

We Want More

I believe many of us would settle for "less" if we knew it meant we could have "more." I'm convinced we'd agree to less of what leaves us feeling numb and flavorless, for more of what thrills our soul; we'd defer to less of what depletes, robs, and exhausts us, to more of what is meaningful, significant, and lasting.

The honest deep-down truth is that we all want our lives to be significant and meaningful, and we want to make an impact and contribute to the people we love and the causes that speak to us. At the same time, we want to know that *we also*, personally matter, and to feel that the activities we involve ourselves in each day matter too.

If we did decide to stop long enough to reflect, we'd have to admit there are some probing questions that plague us, and really, we would like some straightforward answers. For most of us, the questions we'd love to have the simple answers to are not so much the overly-deep, philosophical kind about *the meaning of all life*; not really. It's closer to home than that. We—as intelligent and heart-felt people who can easily get off track in our own journey—want to understand the meaning behind *our life.* The real questions we all wish we had more time to formulate, the right words to voice, more clarity to answer, and enlightened helpers to show us how, are more like these:

"Why am I here, in this particular situation?"
"Am I important to others?"
"How can I make a difference?"
"Why do I feel so lifeless?"
"How can I feel significant and empowered?"
"What's the difference between a calling and a purpose?"

"Can I know mine?"
"What are my specific talents, inborn skills, giftings?"
"On which of my talents, skills, and gifts should I focus?"
"How or where should I use them?"
"What inspires me most?"
"Why does what I care about sometimes make me mad?"
"Are there people I'm not aware of who need my help?"
"Should I feel guilty for wanting work to be inspiring?"
"Where's the line between fun work and being responsible?"
"Should I shift gears in life after all these years?"
"Is it okay to lead with what inspires me most?"
"Am I being selfish?"
"What do I do if I don't know what to do?"
"How do I choose when I'm just not sure?"
"Could I experience greatness?"
"Have I wasted too much time?"
"How do I overcome these insecurities and inhibitions that keep me from being and doing more?"

We think about questions like these from time to time, and sometimes we may give them a lot of attention. Other times, we fully ignore them, perhaps because there's pain, discomfort, confusion, or uncertainty that accompanies them.

Such thoughts are likely coupled with secret desires (that we'd never tell anyone) to be less mundane, less ordinary, less settled, less mediocre, less "asleep" in our day-to-day life. Along with these compelling thoughts, we may feel a

Introduction

deep need, and experience an earnest longing, to be more creative, more expressive, more artistic, more poetic, more emotional, and more connected to the human race.

Ironically, in a day where we "seem" to be incredibly connected and aware, we simply are not, and no matter how accomplished in our life and work we may be, many of us struggle to find a true sense of purpose and meaning, as well as authentic contribution.

What I believe we crave deep in our spirits, is connection that matters—that compels us to look within, then look into the eyes and souls of one another, and consider the things that are honestly and sincerely beautiful and worthy of our attention. Then, we can inhale the greatness of this gift of life, and exhale with fullness of joy.

We Need Some Help

As simple as that seems, it can feel like a mind-boggling concept and look like a complicated process. We need wise mentors and caring helpers to light the path and lead the way, and that's what you will find waiting for you in the pages of this enormously important book.

One chapter at a time, the authors of this book present you with practical yet inspirational guidance and actionable steps to help you live each and every day with a sense of clarity. Their words and intentional direction will help you sort through all the muck, and separate the worthy voices from those that are not worth your time or attention.

Through their exciting lessons and compelling stories, these seven mentors will help you recognize your own amazing value and tremendous power to live fully and to positively impact others. This diverse group includes men and women of various ages and professional backgrounds, who come from many walks of life on their self-discovery journey. They've each traveled a unique path, taking very different steps to get where they are today. Any one of these amazing people would freely admit they've not fully "arrived" at the promises and the destination reserved just for them, but they are all determined to keep charging forward. They are strong because they've learned confidence, and they are clear and convinced about the things they do know for sure. Most importantly, each one has an inspired message and lesson just for you.

Starting today, you can boldly set out on a beautiful treasure hunt, to uncover your purpose and God-given giftings so you can go about the work of bringing your brilliance and splendor to your world of work, business, family, and community. This book can be your catalyst to do the inner work. From there, you can take the outer steps to get going with an inspired life!

It's on! Now is the time to confidently and joyously make the most of the gifts and Godly desires you've been given.

Enjoy!

Margo DeGange

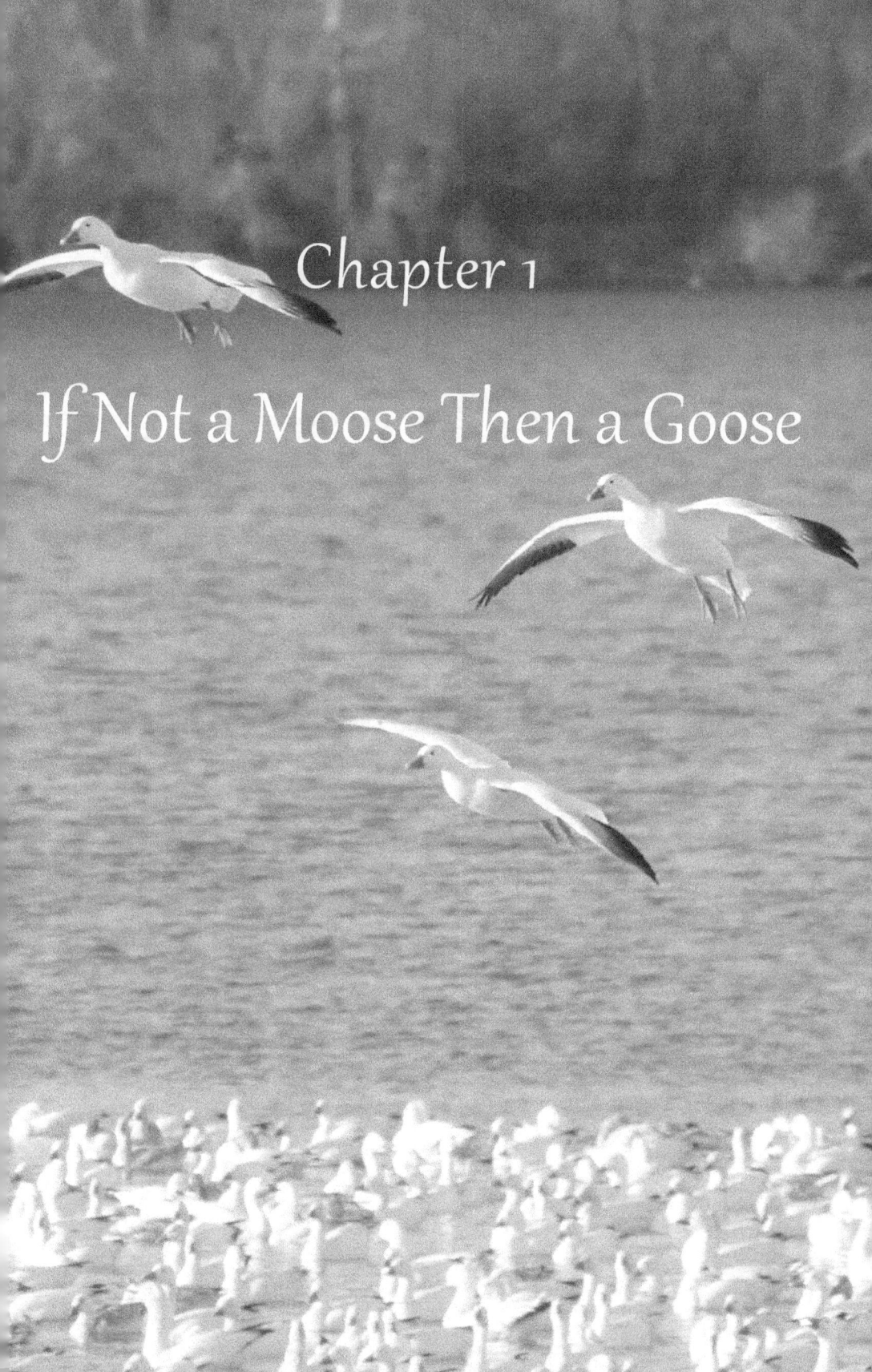

Chapter 1

If Not a Moose Then a Goose

"When we sense that our plan is actually a part of a grander plan, then our actions bring a high sense of worth and value."

                          Timothy Grant Carter

If Not a Moose Then a Goose

Timothy Grant Carter

I have a close friend and mentor in the city in which I live. His name is Ed Lewis and he is an amazing man. He just turned seventy years old and to celebrate, he ran his fiftieth 26-mile marathon. He amazes me on so many levels; spiritually, mentally, philosophically, and philanthropically.

I learn so much from my conversations with Ed. Each of our visits is an adventurous episode of warm sharing, and results in heartfelt learning, and life-enriching growth and personal development. During one of our fireside chats, he related how in a previous trip to Canada, he could not leave until he had seen a moose. Hold on . . . this is not as crazy as it sounds. For him, this moment of connection with nature was imperative. He could not miss this appointment. It was a moment of "discovering his splendor." And true to the man I have come to know, love, and respect, he did indeed see his moose before returning home.

During another fireside chat, Ed described his most recent trip to Canada, during which both he and his wife shared one of these important "needs" of discovery; the pair of them could not return home until they saw a Canadian Wild Goose.

Birds of a feather truly seem to flock together. So he and his wife did not return home until they saw a beautiful flock of geese. Furthermore, they got a very close-up, intimate photograph of three geese landing.

Thinking about this moment of "splendor," I joked with Ed, "*So if not a moose, then a goose!*" I knew I was on to something, as he laughed heartily and said, "*Yes, that's it exactly!*"

I decided this story must be the centerpiece of this chapter. So, here is the account in Ed's own words!

If Not a Moose, then a Goose

My wife Dawn and I have made two trips to Canada in the relatively recent past. (Yes, Ed's wife, like my wife, is named Dawn). *The first was to see Niagara Falls. The second was to run the Niagara Falls Marathon. Somehow, the actual reasons for going got tangled up with animals—and so much more. This is what happened.*

I decided I wanted to take Dawn to Niagara Falls. I had been working hard and she had been tolerating my long hours. We drove. It was a long trip during which time we had ample opportunity to see the land, marvel at the beauty of the country, and enjoy being together. We went to the Canadian side. When we arrived, we were delighted by the falls. There are those mystic types who claim that it's all those positive ions—produced by the water crashing on the rocks—that make us humans so mellow as we stand there gawking at all the misty turmoil. And I could see why the brother of Napoleon— way back in 1804—would ride in a carriage with his new bride for a honeymoon, all the way from New Orleans, and start a destination craze for young lovers that has lasted till this day.

Somehow, after we had looked at the falls for a while, I began to get excited about the prospect of seeing more of the land—of experiencing something different, strange, and perhaps wild. We went down to the local tourist agency, walked in, and I told the young lady working at the desk that I wanted to see a moose before I went home.

It seemed to perplex her. She pondered, then with no answer as to where I might see a moose, she went to ask a co-worker. The co-worker didn't know, so they called someone somewhere else in the tourist hierarchy and asked where I could see a moose. That person didn't know either, but asked around, and called back a few minutes later saying we could see a moose up near Lake Muskoka in central Ontario.

The question arises, why did I want to see a moose? I don't have a very rational answer. I just know that moose are clumsily, comically exotic and worthy of being seen. But more than that, I owed something to the majestic, bearded moose that hung on the wall of my Dad's car dealership when I was a boy. Even as a five year old (or perhaps because I was one), I knew I shared something with that moose and with moose wherever they were to be found; I knew that the moose and I were both children of the same creative force that stirred the pot of creation. Something about being happy and free in a beautiful foreign land made me feel there was a kinship with the wild that took symbolic shape in the form of a moose. It was one of those semi-palpable cravings—a desire for something real, not virtual; for something of flesh and blood, not ones and zeros; perhaps something risky or dangerous that lets you know you and the world are still alive, that your heart can still throb with excitement. It was totally irrational, but compelling, in a similar way that love or moral convictions are irrational but compelling. Seeing a moose was not just a desire, it became a spiritual quest.

We traveled north, sailed around Lake Muskoka on an old coal-fired, steamer mail boat, and finally stumbled on the moose in the wilds of Ontario.

I can't exactly say that the moose we saw really reciprocated my spiritual feelings—in fact, it ducked back into the woods after taking a long look and deciding we were not necessarily to be trusted. But if he was not moved with feelings of spiritual communion, I was. We turned around and drove back home.

This most recent trip was for the purpose of running my fiftieth marathon. My wife says that I am now retired from marathons, being seventy years of age. Time will tell about that. Nevertheless, a young friend suggested that we go on a run from Buffalo, New York to Niagara Falls, crossing the border, and running beside the St. Lawrence River. Knowing the place to be beautiful, I decided I would do it.

Once again, Dawn and I drove to Niagara Falls. Autumn had arrived by the time we departed North Carolina, but the vistas didn't disappoint. Some of the mountains and valleys were colorful and beautiful—some even breath-taking. We arrived at the border, encountering a not-too-smiley border guard who asked lots of questions about whether I had guns in the car, if I owned guns at home, and for what we wanted to visit Canada. Somehow we passed the test and he let us in.

The marathon was great. We ran across and beside the St. Lawrence River on a road that Sir Winston Churchill called, "The prettiest Sunday afternoon drive in the world." We finished right beside the falls. The weather was good (for running). The pain was intense, but temporary; the satisfaction of completion is forever. I finished second in my age group, though I didn't care. It was okay, considering there were only three of us in our seventies still able to totter to the starting line.

Dawn and I are bird watchers. From the first moments of my consideration of the Niagara Falls Marathon, I had been thinking about what kinds of birds we could see. I was given a book from a good friend on great spots to view birds, and found that Niagara Falls was one of them—as long as all you wanted to see were gulls. We saw them. But I wanted more.

I remembered seeing a migratory flight of snow geese years ago in Nebraska. I wanted Dawn to see *and hear that wild experience. I looked for where I could find migrating snow geese. I found that up north of Quebec, a nine-hour drive from Niagara Falls, at a place called Cape Tormente, there were enormous flocks of snow geese. The day after the Marathon, still sore and aching, we left for Quebec.*

I took Spanish . . . they speak French! It was a fascinating trip—almost like Europe. The old city of Quebec still has the fortified wall around it. One can walk around the entire city on top or beside the walls. Below is the St. Lawrence River, with an occasional cruise ship, tanker, sail boat, or barge. It was beautiful. We ate French food; I bumbled with conversation; they laughed; I was excited about the prospect of seeing the snow geese. Then the bad news came. The snow geese had already migrated. They were already in New Jersey. My plans were foiled.

Never one to allow a little bad news to deter me, I wanted to see for myself. We hopped in the car and drove to a beautiful basilica of St. Anne which is an enormous cathedral in the middle of nowhere—but on the way to Cape Tormente, which was where the snow geese had been a couple of weeks earlier. We stopped to marvel at the beautiful church, with its walls covered with crutches and braces from the miraculous cures that had taken place there. We took some pictures, then went on to Cape Tormente.

When we got to there, we found, to our delight, that no one had told the snow geese they were all supposed to be gone. It is our guess that we saw about ten thousand snow geese, feeding on the fields, then taking flight in tremendous, cacophonous flocks, darkening the sky as they went. After we saw them, I was ready to come home.

Why snow geese? Well, there is something so wonderful and inexplicable about that noisy trip they make from the far northern reaches of arctic Canada to the south, and back again. Snow geese don't have big brains, like we do, but they somehow know how to go, where to go, and when to go. They do what birds, animals, and in fact all creatures do, or want to do: meet, mate, raise young, teach them the essentials of life, take them on their first flights, then fly free, together, without map or compass, but also without being lost, to relative warmth and into a timeless future. When they do it, when they all fly—thousands taking flight at a time—they darken the sky, and not only do they fill the air with feathers and wings, but they make as joyful a noise unto the Lord as I have ever heard. I am glad Dawn got to see and hear it. I am glad I got to wave to them, to cheer them—fellow creatures from that same pot of creation that gave me life and breath, eyes to see, and a heart to feel joy. Why snow geese? Because they are my brothers and sisters and they help me celebrate beauty, freedom, and the reality of the community of being.

So, that is Ed's story, and certainly it leads us to important lessons about how to "discover our splendor" in life. These nuggets of destiny do not consist of far-off goals for us to reach. Rather, they are moments of gold that can escape us along our daily path if we are not looking. These fleeting whispers of calling could miss us and pass us by if we get too busy, and if we get too focused on the urgent, instead of the important.

So my powerful point here is to urge you: don't miss the important. Seize the fleeting moments of meaning, without letting them pass you by.

He Leadeth Me

As a Quaker Christian, I am confident that God wants to lead our steps. Moreover, I am convinced that this comes to us more from the inside out than from the outside in, and shows up as "deep knowings," in which it is providentially granted that we can sense, see, and seize our individual "splendor" in life.

The hymnist says: "*He leadeth me, oh blessed thought.*" I am not sure there is a life of splendor without this deep knowing. When we sense that our plan is actually a part of a grander plan, then our actions bring a high sense of worth and value.

This fits into what Colossians 1:27 reveals as a solid foundation for a life of significance. It is His life in me that makes my fleeting steps have lasting meaning. Psalms 23 talks about a shepherd leading our lives. This sense of His design and touch can add great serenity and purpose to our lives. Spirituality can give us amazing, deeper dimension in our day-to-day existence. Plugging into the divine plan is critical to this sense of meaning.

Realizing when we are out of step is actually a great part of moving in step. We can sense when something is "out of whack," and change the channels back so we are receptive to our spiritual calling. We can learn to make this deeper dimension a solid and sure part of our lives, and in so doing, even the common-place becomes a moment of "splendor."

Competence

Once we have a foundation that helps us see our own significance, then we can move forward with greater courage and confidence in our own ability. Personal competence is not egoism. Competence makes people relax around us. Who'd want to get on a plane with a pilot who hoped he could fly?

Our development of legitimate abilities leads us to increased confidence, which will make others around us sense our strength and want to be a part of our endeavors. This commitment to personal excellence is a great foundation for leadership, and it is a true mark that we have sensed our "splendid" calling.

Personal Truth

I often wonder if Shakespeare realized when he had his character, Polonius, say the words, *"To thine own self be true,"* that he was penning words that would shape minds for hundreds of years to come. And these words have shaped minds for obvious reasons. They are on target for human growth and welfare. Instinctive hunches must be celebrated and fine-tuned so we can grow in a commitment to our personal truth. Still, even when we have a deep realization of our calling, it's possible that we miss it if we do not face ourselves and own up to difficult truths about our personal lives.

Quite a few years ago, I named my blog *Guts is the Key* (I call my blog posts BEAMS). There is quite a story behind this, but suffice it to say I had a deep realization that it was going to take unusual courage to accomplish my goals in life. One thing that is invariably true about courage is that it takes "guts" to affect important change. Even if we have a sense of true knowing about our mission in life, it is not likely to come to pass without courageous resolve and willingness to accept the truth about ourselves.

The story is told of a senior citizen who was driving down the freeway when his wife called his cell phone saying, *"Joe, I just heard on the news there's a car going the wrong way on Route 20. Please be careful!"* Joe responded with a certain urgency, saying, *"It's not one car, it's hundreds of them!"*

The truth that is hardest for us to see is the truth about ourselves. It is only when we face ourselves candidly that we can move on to discover the splendor in our lives, and experience our own deep sense of calling and mission.

Patience and Persistence

Often, when people discover their life's true path and find the courage to face themselves, the natural desire is to want to get there right away. Yet the truth is, there are no shortcuts to excellence. Splendor is only found in the patient pursuit of right and truth. The practice of doing the next right thing must be continual and steadfast. Courage, character, and faith never cheat nor cut corners.

Once we find the vigor and stream of life's good path for us, just getting our toes wet will not do. We must intentionally stay in the flow of the river of our highest purpose to find its highest fulfillment. The drop of water only finds its meaning in the current of the river or the ocean.

My friend Ha Tran called me when she was concerned that I was going to give up and sell short my plans for the future. She urged me, *"Tim, you have created a track to run on; now you must run on it."* We must practice herculean follow through to see our dreams come to pass. If not a Moose, then a goose, but we must certainly stay on the track.

Selfishness

When you have this essence of calling going in the right direction, the last thing you should want to do is spoil it with selfishness. Selfishness is like the drop of ink that can cloud the clarity of all the water in the sink. Selfishness is like a hole in the radiator that lets all the water drain out. The foundation that keeps us on the right track of our calling is a faith that finds a higher power. For me, Christ is my higher power.

Self is a poor final authority for life direction. Humility that works through faith and that manifests through love and service, is a better foundation for a life's work and mission.

Service is like a stop-leak fluid that plugs the leak selfishness forms.

The inquisitive eyes of a child are much more in tune to see the wonder, magic, amazement, and meaning around us, than are the eyes of pride and egotistical pomp.

Growth

When a good foundation is intact and in place, growth is necessary. Growing is the proof of meaning, and the kind of growth we need is the growth that happens through gratefulness, acceptance, and celebration. Counting your blessings will fill you with a happy and helpful feeling of well-being. Gratefulness inspires a healthy sense of mission. Acceptance finds serenity in the mission. Have you ever seen a Robin fret over whether it should build its nest?

My mother had an incredible capacity to make a joyful celebration out of the simple and every day things. To Louise Carter, daily duties were a ritual of great happiness and value. She embraced—not dreaded—the tasks that most people considered mundane.

Acceptance grows like a robin's work into a healthy life of meaning. It builds its nest of meaning that finds its expression in celebration—celebration that starts today and goes with us wherever we go. Our healthy sense of work and mission will be manifest by a life of joy, in every situation. Ideal *outlooks* are more reliable than ideal circumstances! Discover the splendor in your own healthy attitude.

Aim High

Last but not least, the way to find the moose and to go on and find the goose is to find the wonderful dear life around us in every situation. Having this kind of complete success in finding your calling requires that you aim high!

Life is a one shot deal. A quarter wrapper is designed to be worth ten dollars, but until it's filled with quarters it's worth nothing. It takes courage to fill in our potential, because when people see that we're worth something, we have further to fall. People will try to shoot you down to be on their level (there is great truth in the old saying, "*misery loves company*"), but like the quarter wrapper, design is marked all over our nature. It is evident that we were made for something valuable and meaningful, but we have to fill the wrapper of our lives with the right thing in order to attain the value and purpose for which we were designed.

Don't forget my friend Ed's search for the moose and his subsequent search for the goose. Look for the wonderful moments of beauty and loveliness in your own life. Do not settle for less and let these magic moments pass you by. Find your own wild calling and incredible fulfillment! Discover your splendor in life.

About Timothy Grant Carter, a.k.a. "Slam"

Timothy Grant Carter, the positive, fiery, and highly sought-after, inspirational speaker who helps individuals as well as organizations "Springboard to Significance," is a career catalyst and award-winning sales professional whose stellar work is recognized and applauded both internationally and in the USA. He is a best-selling author whose wit and keen insights have his readers consistently asking for more. He's the fun creator of the popular blog articles called "Beams." Each Beam is captivating, entertaining, and full of useful tips and top-notch information to help entrepreneurs and career professionals own their significance.

Timothy is well-known in business circles as "SLAM," for his no-nonsense approach to life and work. A popular and motivating keynote speaker and sales trainer, he knows how to effectively connect with audiences and inspire them for results. He empowers others with original sayings and visionary insight, and his hundreds of speaking engagements include many Christian messages, and multitudes of keynotes and sales presentations in the corporate environment.

He is the author of the best-selling book, *Positive x Positive = Unlimited*, and his rare business insight was featured in the book, *25 Brilliant Business Mentors*. He was also an author in the source book for speakers, *25 Brilliant Speakers*. SLAM knows how to inspire audiences to take action, and individuals to create meaningful and successful lives!

Website: *GutsIsTheKey.com*

Chapter 2

Your "Gift of Brilliance"

"Trust the changing of the seasons and the creator who changes them on your behalf."

Margo DeGange

Your "Gift of Brilliance"

Margo DeGange

I grew up on Long Island. As a child I loved interior design. I used to draw floor plans and think of new and creative ways to arrange my bedroom and make it magical through the elements and principles of design. I was constantly scouring swap shops and garage sales for cool pieces that would help revolutionize my space. I was one of those children who absolutely loved interior design.

I was definitely a creative type, but in college, my deeper calling of "inspirational teacher" started to surface. I became a mentor to others. My desire was always to encourage people and help them find direction for their lives, maybe because that's what I wanted most as a kid.

Before I was able to finish college, I got married, and within three years I had three kids! When my youngest child was one, I started a career in decorating in the niche of children's design. It seemed easier than going back to school; I already had a natural knack for design, I could earn money almost immediately, and work from home to start. I had a sewing machine just sitting there, and I could learn what I needed to know as I went along.

I created a line of custom baby bedding, sewing most of the pieces myself. They spanned the range from amusingly whimsical to stately and elegant. I was quite successful in that niche and I quickly added bedroom design for all ages. In no time flat I was filling orders from cradle to king! That led to window fashions, upholstery, slipcovers, color consultation, redesign, and more. Through solid customer care and great marketing, my reputation grew, and it wasn't long before I was speaking at international design shows in the areas of business, marketing, and design. I also consulted design professionals from around the world.

My speaking and consulting took off in two distinct directions: speaking to other design professionals on business and design topics, and speaking to homeowners on interior design and lifestyle topics. I began building curriculum and educational programs to more formally train others, and I became skilled at content creation and digital products creation.

To substantiate my speaking and training, I went back to school and completed a bachelor's degree in leadership and communication, and a master's degree in adult education and instructional design. I also earned a degree in speech communications and several certificates: human behavior, behavior and personality assessments, online training, home fashions design, and color consulting.

Eventually I was speaking on topics pertaining to life in general: what makes us feel significant, how we can connect with others, how to discover our gifts and calling, how to set up our homes for success, how to spark our creative genius, and more. This was not just about design and business anymore, this was about life.

Over the years, I did develop many talents (some through great effort and pain), but every time I got on stage to speak, teach, or train—no matter how big or small the audience—I knew I was tapping into my core gift. Audiences knew it too. They could feel my heart. They sensed I sincerely cared about them as individuals; that I was there to encourage, inspire, and uplift people in their spirit.

What We All Want

What I noticed repeatedly in my work was that so many people were frustrated because they lacked clear direction about their life and life-work. Regardless of their vocation or avocation—whether speakers, business coaches, ministers, receptionists, lawyers, interior designers, or stay-at-home parents, people desperately needed help either getting started in meaningful life-work, getting clear on a direction, or navigating the changes that naturally come at different stages and seasons of life. I was drawn to help them.

After almost thirty years of working with individuals and business people from all over the world, I know that what we all want deep in our souls is to create lives of significance, connect with others in purposeful and meaningful ways, and express the gifts that are within us.

Today my work takes on many forms. Mainly I speak to audiences, publish books, and write. I also lead a non-profit organization I founded with a small seed of faith back in 1999.

Through Women of Splendor, I challenge people to get clear and identify what's important, and to find an authentic sense of personal expression in their lives, then I help them to pick up the mantle and in turn inspire and empower others.

My "Gift of Brilliance"

My "Gift of Brilliance" is helping others find their "Gift of Brilliance" for this season of their life. Now I'm going to show you how to discover yours, too! Let's Begin.

Stumbling and Struggling for Purpose

People today seem to be pulled in many directions with a lack of focus, often feeling insignificant and struggling to find a sense of real purpose. We all want to enjoy meaningful life-work that is right for us and that helps us to contribute to something bigger than just, "me."

Have you ever wondered what you were put in this world to do? Have you thought maybe there was just one thing you should focus on, only to get confused with your many skills, natural talents, and interests?

With so many options around us, finding our calling and even our brilliance can seem difficult and overwhelming, but it doesn't have to be. You *can* discover that "Gift of Brilliance" that helps you connect meaningfully and powerfully with others.

In the pages that follow, I'll take you through the steps to understand and find your calling, your gifts, your passion, and your "Gift of Brilliance." You will never be confused about it again!

Your Heavenly Calling and Purpose: A Given

First and foremost, our *foundational* calling is to love and serve God. That's our "heavenly calling." I think of it like this: God is "calling." He is calling each of us to get to know Him better and to love Him more. He's the one doing the "calling." He's "ringing you up"! We also all have one major *foundational* purpose, and that is to love others. These concepts are a given. So with that in mind, and for the sake of clarity, let's just assume we know this, and talk from this point on in terms of your calling and purpose being what you are here on earth to be and do, and what you are seeking to discover.

Your Core Calling

At the same time that He is calling you to be with Him, He is also calling you to *be* someone (a *someone* who has things to *do*). Often, this part of the calling comes from the desires in your heart that long to be expressed outwardly.

We hear a lot of talk about our "calling" in terms of something we should *do*—such as a type of life-work or an activity in our day-to-day life. I see it differently. I know there are certainly things for us to do, but that comes later. Our calling is not something we *do*; it is something we *are*.

As we walk this earth, we each have a core calling. Your core calling is always there, has always been there, and will always be there with you. It is part of your DNA! The way you express your calling may change, but the core of it remains.

Discovery

To get to your core calling, you will have to go on a discovery journey! It does take some effort, but it's not difficult, and it's fully worth it because you will learn a key concept about yourself when you do.

The key to unveiling your core calling is to consider who you are at the very base of your being. Don't look at the things you do, rather, look at who you are in terms of the *human component*.

You'll do this by reflecting: by asking yourself a number of questions, by journaling, by noticing what attributes you are portraying when time seems to stand still (or fly by), and by recognizing what role you're playing when you light up, come alive, or jump to action! You'll also begin to unveil it by choosing words to describe who you *are* (more on that later).

Your calling is not *what* you do, as in *"I'm called to be a doctor,"* or "I'm called to be a lawyer," or *"I'm called to be a school teacher."* You might be *directed to do* those things once you know your calling, but your calling is even deeper—much richer than that! (The things we do are simply *ways* that we express our calling.)

Again, your calling is really *who you are at your core*—and who you are at your core is not a school teacher, a plumber, a singer, or a business person, because obviously those careers and roles were all created by men and women. Who you are at your core involves how you function, act, or perform; it's greater than what you *do* at any given time in your life (you can *do* a lot of things without *being* the person you were called to be. That's why your core calling underlies everything else, and is deeper than the *things* you are directed to do).

You can think of your calling as that "thing" that's fully aligned with who you are, but in a more profound sense, it is who you are at your very core, and that rarely if ever changes. It will begin to make sense when you ask yourself questions like:

"Who am I as a person?"
"What do I come to this world to do?"
"What drives me?"
"What do I care about in the world?"
"What makes me mad in the world?"
"How do I connect with others emotionally?"
"Where's my connecting point?"
"Which human emotions do I feel most connected to?"
"What attributes did I come to this world to express?"
"How do I connect with others on an interpersonal plane?"

Now let's get to the meat of it (how exciting)! Your calling might "sound" something like this:

"I'm a connector."
"I'm a helper."
"I'm an encourager."
"I'm a communicator."
"I'm an inspirer."
"I'm a motivator."
"I'm a healer."
"I am a repair of the breach."
"I'm a problem-solver."
"I'm an idea person."

A woman who interviewed me discovered that she was a mirror (she was a life coach by trade). She excitedly said, *"I'm a mirror!"*

Once you define it, you may want to add an adjective or two to further express your core calling in terms of *your* personal truth:

"I am a creator of beauty."
"I'm an inspirational teacher."
"I am an expressive edifier."
"I'm an inspirational creator of beauty" (see the extra word there?)

These are ways in which we behave, and we do it quite naturally, so much so that we can easily overdo it, almost as though others have to say to us, "*Alright already, stop communicating!*" or, "*Enough now, quit trying to motivate me!*" We are so comfortable being "that" because it is truly who we are. It's really in our spirit. You just can't help but be it, in other words, you can't *not* be it!

I'm sure you're starting to get it now. The exciting part of this journey is that once we understand who we are at our core, we will discover there are many ways to express that core calling. This is where we have been given a lot of freedom and liberty, and of course we always have the privilege of asking God to lead our steps each and every day as we walk out our calling and purpose.

So when it comes down to it, your core calling is really not about you, it's about that bigger part! It's about God *in* you!

Brilliant Action Step:

Take out a sheet of paper and jot down all kinds of words and phrases to describe yourself, aiming for those that best express who you are at your core and what emotional actions you came to do (not activities). Then, from the many words on the page, create a phrase (two or three words at most) to describe your "core calling" (mine is "inspirational teacher/mentor"). You can always change your phrase if you discover later that another group of words better describes who you are at your core.

Gifts, Skills, Talents, Passions, Experience

As we go through life, we are naturally drawn to a variety of industries and events that appeal to that core calling in us (who we are). Over time, we become "well-rounded." We sign up for many different programs and courses. We experience a variety of service roles, jobs, and careers. We read a wide range of books, we gravitate towards a slew of interests, and we participate in an array of activities and hobbies. Because of this, we develop a plethora of gifts, skills, talents, passions, and experience in many areas over time. On top of this, we play a variety of life and business roles like mother, father, manager, counselor, and mentor. This is what I mean in my talks when I refer to us being "many-faceted human beings."

Then, for whatever reason (probably because of the self-help hype and buzz-words flying around), we come to a place in our lives where we feel we must suddenly be crystal clear on that *one thing* we *do* to explain to others *who we are* (and gosh-forbid it should change). So we mistakenly try to define our identity around things we do (usually some kind of occupational label: doctor, interior designer, content marketer, publisher). That's fine for marketing a business, but not so great for knowing who you are!

What if, on the other hand, we allowed ourselves to identify first and foremost with our core calling (inspirational teacher, motivator, encourager, problem-solver, repairer of the breach)? We could lead with that, and it would open the door to many creative ways to demonstrate that calling at any point in time. We would no longer feel compelled to jam all of our interests into one pigeon hole, leaving out the ones that don't "fit." Suddenly, we are the "healer" who happens to be practicing medicine *at this time*, or the "inspirational teacher" who is *currently* facilitating seminars, or the "creative connector" who is running for office *this year*. We are getting close to the "Gift of Brilliance!"

We get quite confused about what we should do with our lives because we are brainwashed into thinking we *must* define who we are by what we *do*.

We also get confused about what we should do with our lives because we picked up all these gifts, skills, talents, passions, and experiences along the way, and it dawns on us that we are actually good at *many* things! Yet we have told ourselves we have to select *just one* with which to identify for *life*! In terms of knowing who you are, that is the *wrong approach*!

Your "Gift of Brilliance"

Once we understand our core calling, we can start to look at where our "Gift of Brilliance" lies.

Your "Gift of Brilliance" isn't being a communicator, or a healer, or an inspirer—remember, *that's your calling, and that supersedes everything!*

Your "Gift of Brilliance" is how you *express* your core calling *at this time in your life*, and there are many ways you can express it. The expression of your calling will be based on your experience, your skills sets, your passions, what you're naturally good at, and where you are on your life's path.

So let's say you're an inspirational teacher (your core calling), for example. You could express that by being a school teacher, you could express it by being a life coach, you could express it by being a team-leader for a franchise group, you could express it as a motivational speaker, and you could express it teaching art to grade-school children. There are so many beautiful and worthy ways to express it!

Different Seasons of Your "Gift of Brilliance"

There are definite season in your life. A season might last one year, or it could last five or ten. Your "Gift of Brilliance" in one season of your life may be very different from your "Gift of Brilliance" in another. Personally, I had very distinct seasons where only one part of my work took center stage. I didn't freak out about it, nor did I lose those skills with which I was *not* leading. I just understood it was a time to go forward strongly in only one area. This was in part due to a clear leading in my spirit from God, and in part from the right doors opening (which is likely the same thing).

For a time I led with interior design, for a time I led with marketing consultation, and for a time I led as a content publisher. It's not that there was a grand finale' for the "Gift of Brilliance" from which I was moving away; I simply felt a shift in my heart that came on slowly and picked up speed.

Your "Gift of Brilliance" for this season is that thing you desire to do (have passion for) right now in your life, and at which you are also especially skilled. It's also something to which other people respond positively. In addition, it's something that is underwritten by your core calling (that thing you *are*, such as a "problem solver," "expresser of beauty," or "inspirational teacher."

How to Find Your "Gift of Brilliance" for *This* Season— *An Exercise:*

To find your "Gift of Brilliance" for this season of your life, all you have to do is get out some paper. On one sheet, make a list of all the things you are especially good at doing. Include everything you are good at and everything others think you are good at even if you don't enjoy doing them.

On another sheet of paper, make a list of everything you are passionate about, even if you are not good at that thing.

    This is where some people get confused, because you can be really good at something and *not* be passionate about it. You may have done a job for so long, or even have a natural gift to do something well, but not thoroughly enjoy doing it. You have the knack but not the love. It's even worse when others recognize your definite skill, and continually tell you, "*You're so good at this.*" Well-meaning friends and family members may even tell you, "*I think you should open your own business and do this for a living. You'll make a lot of money.*"

    Then there's the person who is extremely passionate about something they're just not skilled at doing, and no one can get through to them that they should drop it like a hot flapjack. We all know that guy or gal who loves to sing in the shower but couldn't hold a tune if it were sitting in a wash bucket, or that eager beagle who feels *"Called to play drums on the worship team,"* and is constantly frustrated with rejection slips, when he could just find something that works better for him—and others! That drummer's calling is likely "to inspire others" and there are many ways to do that. Playing the drums is likely not one of them. Others will recognize your gifts!

Back to the lists:

*From the "good at" list, go back and circle the three or four things at which you are most skilled, and from the "passionate at" list, circle the three or four things you have the most passion towards. Now, look for the place where those circles overlap, and "BLING," therein lies your "Gift of Brilliance" for this season of your life—where you have a tremendous skill **and** a great passion.*

Get creative to find a way the two can be implemented together in some form of community service, business, or self expression. Adjust as necessary. Remember, you have freedom in the meadow!

You can spend this season of your life doing something you are good at but not passionate for, or something you are full of passion for but not very good at, and you can spin your wheels not feeling thoroughly ignited and successful. Or, you can uncover that "Gift of Brilliance" for *this* life's season (however long or short), and focus your energies on that exquisite place where your greatest skill intersects with your greatest passion. Once you do, you—and those you serve—will never be quite the same!

A man's gift makes room for him, and brings him before great men (Proverbs 18:16, NKJV). So will your "Gift of Brilliance." If you're seriously skilled and contagiously passionate in an area, others will call you on it!

Get Creative

If you feel you have more than one major interest and more than one major passion, get creative and design something new and innovative around them. Play with it. See how your gifts from one industry can be used in another, or how one style of music can enhance another genre. It's *your* "Gift of Brilliance," make it shine.

Don't Want to Choose Just One Focus Area?

Think of it this way, when you were in high school preparing for the prom, you had to choose one outfit to wear. When you went to the dealership to buy a car, you had to choose one car. There were many you could've chosen—many you loved, but you had to choose. You had to leave something behind. You may have even toiled over two or three before your final decision, but ultimately you had to make that brutal choice. Once you made it, you settled it in your heart and went forward.

Pick it, put it on, wear it fully, and forget the one you didn't choose. You are only able to wear one at a time. Don't waste time second guessing—that just takes all of your power from you. As long as it's in line with your core calling, wear it as if there is no other option and go forward with it. If a year in, you see it's not working, then make the change, but give it a fair chance without the possibility of distraction. Once you decide on your course of action, give yourself a time allotment to see it though, and make it long enough to see some results—a year might be the bare minimum.

As you grow, change, develop, and evolve, you will leave one "Gift of Brilliance" for another, but your many skills and talents will remain a part of you. The passions too, from which you move away, will always hold interest for you. They just won't continue to be where you shine your brightest; they may even become opportunities for delegation or building a team, so others can oversee your former endeavors. It's your choice. Just be willing to let go of the old to embrace the new when the new season approaches. Trust the changing of the seasons and the creator who changes them on your behalf!

Your Seasons May Lead to Something Big

Sometimes, you do one thing in Season #1, another thing in Season #2, and a third thing in Season #3 (like I did), because in season #4, all of these gifts and skills will be needed and called upon to be used together.

That's how it is for me right now with Women of Splendor, my non-profit organization. Women of Splendor includes mentoring, meaningful life work, coursework, curriculum writing, speaking, publishing, event planning, marketing, creative expression, the arts, and even interior design and décor'. Everything I have done throughout my career is being used now in my leadership of Women of Splendor, and it's quite magnificent to see. Nothing is wasted. I could never have known that from the beginning, and along the way I often questioned this winding garden path I was taking, but now I see why.

I formed and registered Women of Splendor back on January 8, 1999 and I knew then it was for the future, but I didn't know precisely when I would run with it. It was a seed planted in my heart by God almost twenty years ago. I didn't launch it officially until May 25, 2012, and that's because it wasn't the time; it wasn't the season. Yet the preparation for that season was happening all along the way. All those other seasons, occupations, skills, experiences, and "Gifts of Brilliance" I was involved in through the years were for a purpose. It's a good thing I didn't listen to my doubts (at least not for too long). Here I am today, understanding the plan more clearly than I ever have—and likely not as clearly as I will in the future.

We serve a perfect God who partners with imperfect people to bring out the glory He placed in us. He made us to be creative, expressive, useful, and passionate, and to experience different seasons of excitement and jubilation that are often mixed with questions and uncertainty. It's all part of the glorious ride to our ultimate, "Gift of Brilliance."

About Margo DeGange

Margo DeGange, M.Ed., is a business & lifestyle designer, and the founder and President of Women of Splendor. She's an international best-selling author and inspirational speaker with a witty and engaging way of helping us see everyday life with greater clarity and meaning. Margo empowers audiences to embrace their God-given calling in practical ways in life, business, ministry, and community. She presents a variety of personal and professional growth topics to help us discover our gifts and engage in significant life-work that positively impacts others. She's helped individuals worldwide ditch the distractions and get focused on what personally matters most to them, so they can fulfill their God-given desires and purpose.

A human behavior consultant and a master degreed adult learning expert, Margo teaches and mentors from a faith-based perspective, understanding what motivates us to move beyond mere success into lives of significance and true joy. She's been a passionate entrepreneur for almost thirty years, with various businesses in wholesale and retail sales, seminars & training, business consulting, interior design, and print & digital publishing. She's hosted events, conferences, and seminars across the country and abroad, and served on a variety of boards and panels for the betterment of her industries. Upon request, Margo hosts the life-transforming *4 Seasons of Success* conferences in various churches and organizations, and she publishes the *Women of Splendor Magazine* twice yearly.

Website: *MargoDeGange.com*

Chapter 3

This is Your Decade

"*I am God's masterpiece, His greatest work. This revelation has transformed me forever.*"

Dorothy-Inez Del Tufo

This is Your Decade

Dorothy-Inez Del Tufo

After graduating from college at the age of forty, I made one of the biggest decisions of my life; I quit my high paying corporate job to pursue my childhood dream of becoming a makeup artist. Talk about scary. As a sales manager, I played Les Brown's motivational talk, "This Is Your Decade," for every employee that joined my team, to set the tone of my working environment. I had played it so many times, I could recite it word for word.

Then one day, I finally heard what Les was saying *for myself* when he asked, *"What hopes and dreams have you put on the shelf of your heart?"* He went on to ask, *"Did you know the richest place on the planet is the graveyard, because so many people die with their ideas, never bringing them to life?"* The thought of dying and not knowing if I could have made it did something to my soul. Something clicked inside of me and I had to know; I had to know if I could make it.

Finally! After nearly a decade of playing that VCR tape, I "heard" what he was saying. I didn't want to make the graveyard any richer with my great ideas. I didn't want to be one of those people who would sit out on the porch rocking back and forth saying, *"I wish I would have tried _____"* (fill in the blank). I always inspired the people I led to be their best self and go for their dreams, yet I was not following my own. Like many people, I was stuck in fear. The time had come for me to fulfill my life's purpose and passion of helping women show up with beauty and confidence.

Trust Him

The journey to where I am today was not an easy one. My husband and I are a military family. Shortly after I quit my corporate job to start my career in beauty, the army moved us from Colorado to North Carolina. I was very angry and suffered from depression. One rainy night, I decided to have my husband help me find the MAC Cosmetics counter at the mall. I decided the enemy was not going to have the victory in my life through depression. I was going to trust God and get into action.

We arrived at the mall just minutes before closing. I was in a baseball cap and sweat pants, and I was not wearing makeup. Heck, I wasn't going to meet anyone right? Wrong! This was a lesson about being ready for an opportunity at all times, because you never know who you are going to meet.

I found the MAC counter attended by a woman who was working alone. I struck up a conversation as she organized the eye shadows. While we spoke, an inner voice kept saying to me, *"Ask her if she is hiring."* I thought,

"*No, I don't even look like a makeup artist.*" Two more times that voice said, "*Ask her if she is hiring.*" Me being the faith-filled woman that I am, said, "*Okay!*" So I timidly said, "*I know I don't look like a makeup artist, but I was wondering if you are hiring.*" She looked up out of the corner of her eye and said, "*As a matter of fact, I am.*" My heart was racing. I had no idea she was the hiring manager. I immediately followed up, and interviewed a few days later. I expected an answer on Wednesday. Wednesday came and in my mind was gone, but at 8:34 pm my phone lit up! The manager from MAC was calling, and she offered me the job. It was like winning a Grammy! I had tried working for MAC in Denver for five years and never got a chance. This was another moment of God showing me that I made the right decision. He was saying, "*Dorothy-Inez, trust me.*" I have always had a faith in God, but this was just the beginning.

Shortly after being hired, my husband was assigned to a base in Kansas. I had to make a decision to leave the job I had dreamed of for most of my adult life or move to Kansas. After much deliberation, my husband and I agreed that I would stay behind. Our hope was that I could transfer in six months even though the odds were against us. The store in Kansas was fifty-five miles away from where we lived, and the store representative said they rarely had openings, but you know how God is. He makes a way when there seems to be no way, and in less than three months, a position came open. However, now I was faced with another issue. MAC did not allow transfers for employees with less than six months in a position, but guess what? An exception was made! When we trust God with our life, He promises things will work out for our good. For two years, I drove fifty-five miles each way to work, in order to live out my dream. I was unstoppable and this was the catalyst for the next nine years of my decade.

Confront Pain

Fast forward to 2010 in Savannah, Georgia. I am starting over for the second time on this quest to live my dream. This time my husband was deployed to Iraq. Like many women, my whole life revolved around him, especially since we don't have children. It had been about a week in, when I found myself in the deepest depression I had ever experienced. I had no friends or family close by, and I felt the pain of being lonely and of realizing I had lost myself along the way. The woman who had once "appeared" to be confident and independent, found herself lying on a bed crying, as the feelings of abandonment and loneliness she felt as the three-year-old girl—whose mother left her behind—came rushing back. All those years I thought her leaving had never affected me, but there I was: alone, with no distractions, and confronted with what I held deep inside. I cried for hours calling out for my dad and grandma to rescue me, until I got so tired I could cry no more.

It may sound like a sad story but it's not! I am so thankful for that moment because it changed my life. I woke up the next morning with a sense of freedom; I felt cleansed.

Instead of hiding from my pain I was going to confront it. Within thirty days, I had hired a life coach to guide me through my professional development, started belly dancing to get my sexy back, got a karaoke machine to sing my heart out because I always wanted to be a star, and hired a counselor to help heal the pain. I was going to use this time alone to discover who I was. This time was a gift from God so I wasn't wasting a moment. I have learned that we as women are good at taking care of others and forget to take care of ourselves.

Going from beauty to brilliance can happen for anyone including you. Transforming my life required me to realize I was broken and needed healing. I had to be open to hear and receive the truth; the truth that I am created in the image and likeness of God. I am God's masterpiece, His greatest work. This revelation has transformed me forever.

Love Yourself

I have come to realize that every time I criticize myself, I am criticizing the creator and His great creation. I have learned to love myself, for I am His. Loving myself doesn't mean I am selfish—as many of us have been taught. When we truly love and honor ourselves, we can do the same more beautifully for others. The scripture tells us to, *"Love your neighbor as you love yourself."* God knows we can't give what we don't ourselves have. When you love yourself, you have healthy boundaries, healthy relationships, and most of all a healthy you. Honoring the beauty of you inside and out allows you to honor the beauty in others, which also comes from God.

Almost exactly a decade later, I have become a well-known beauty expert, inspirational speaker and best-selling author. It took courage to say *"Yes"* to the vision, perseverance, and of course allowing God to be the driver. When you keep your eyes on Him, nothing is impossible because He will make a way when you think there is no way. Make this your decade!

About Dorothy-Inez Del Tufo

Dorothy-Inez, (said together), also known as the Minister of Beauty, is on a mission to help women show up in their personal and professional lives with confidence and beauty so they can create the lifestyle and income they desire.

Dorothy-Inez had a successful corporate career leading top-performing sales and service teams for over twenty years. She has coached hundreds of professionals on image and brand management. After years of helping others, she felt a deep calling to pursue her own God-inspired goals and dreams.

Today, Dorothy-Inez is a licensed beauty expert, speaker, international best-selling author, and personal development coach. Currently, she is actively pursuing a master's degree in organizational psychology.

Website: *DorothyInez.com*

Chapter 4

From Here to There—
A Birthday Epiphany

"The beautiful aspect of an abundant life is the ability to pass on blessings to others."

Virginia Kettler

From Here to There—
A Birthday Epiphany

Virginia Kettler

The tell-tale flaming candles on the colorful purple and lime-green birthday cake were bright and plentiful. Exactly sixty candles were burning, and they were all mine. I gulped and decided to blow them all out at once, hopefully making it appear to my celebrating friends that I was not only vibrant, but much younger than someone who had experienced six decades of birthdays. Instead of one breath, it took me three to extinguish the flames. We laughed as I cut the cake, all the while I was reminiscing in my head about past birthdays and milestones. Some say birthdays are major life events; I agree with this to a certain extent. It's about the years and miles traveled (or shall I say experiences) more than it is about the birthday event itself.

To be honest, I began my life analysis some time after my fifty-ninth birthday. Looking back, I thought I was unique in doing so, but I've come to realize that taking stock of one's life and accomplishments—or lack thereof—at this age, is common. Not that this "ah-ha" moment changes anything; but it's good to know. I'm probably more mainstream in many respects than I thought.

Knowing

I believe God put a "knower" inside each one of us. It translates into a passion, a type of understanding that drives us in our lives. The key to the "knower" is unlocking how we are to use it. You and I are gifted with incredible, specific talents put in us by our loving God of the universe. His incredible plans for us were laid before we were ever conceived! We possess our individual talents so that we can live a life of destiny and purpose. We are to fulfill a calling—our own—within our lifetime, and fulfilling this calling and purpose is the most satisfying journey one could ever endeavor to take. We were made by our creator to never be satisfied with our life unless we are on the journey set out by Him.

How Do I Know?

The passion we possess is usually a key to our calling and purpose. I remember sitting in a large sanctuary in 1993 in Houston, Texas. I was attending a Christian conference that weekend, and was listening to one of the speakers, Pastor Rick Godwin from San Antonio, Texas. He was talking about excellence in our lives and our God-given passion. His point was to ask yourself about your true passions; what are they? What "gets your blood boiling" in a good way? What things make you cry or feel true compassion? What things excite or speak to you? I sat there pondering, asking myself if I had any idea what my passions were. I absolutely loved horses and animals in every way. I loved helping people. But beyond that, what was it? Rick's explanation of pursuing your passion was even more astounding to me; if I pursued my passion, what God has for me, I will be the very best at that thing. The reason I will be the best, better than anyone in that pursuit, is because God created me to have those individual, specific talents to fulfill that purpose. No two people are alike, no two callings are alike, and no two life journeys are alike. The freeing part of this is that I realized there were no boundaries to pursuing what God has instilled in me. I couldn't let what I saw as barriers—real or imagined—stop me. At that moment I had the deep understanding that if I pursued His calling for me, He would make a way even when there seemed to be no way. Bingo! Many limitations or obstacles we perceive are in our attitudes. It's time for the journey of faith to begin!

Reacting

I felt liberated as I sat in the sanctuary; I had an understanding of what I needed to do. I realized that for as long as I could remember, I enjoyed real estate, every aspect of it. As a young child I watched my parents invest in and own properties. At the time of that meeting, I was a municipal purchasing manager, and didn't know how I would ever transition to real estate. But I knew being in real estate sales was one of my passions. At the same time I recalled being a sales person from the time I was very young. I was always selling something to someone, and something I believed in whole-heartedly, too. If I thought it was worthwhile, I would want it for myself as well. I naturally felt I was helping others by telling them about a valuable product or service.

Tied in with this was an intense desire to help people fulfill their dreams of security and home ownership. The interesting thing was that I could actually make a good living and fulfill my primary passions simultaneously. At that moment, I made a decision to pursue my dream.

Acting

While I finally knew what I wanted to do, I accepted it would start with baby steps. This meant taking classes, researching brokerages, discussing options, and listening to solid, sage advice. Within two years after taking the required classes, I passed the state licensing exam and officially became a Realtor. I worked on a part-time basis for eight years gaining valuable experience while still holding my full-time purchasing position. I ultimately retired from purchasing to pursue my passion full-time, working for different brokerages. In 2005 my best friend Brenda Watson and I started our own company, Sherlock Realtors. Finally in 2008 I finished my brokerage classes and achieved my real estate broker's license.

Looking back over those years before real estate I discovered that God positioned me to reach that place, at that time. My experiences with work, friends, family, and church all played key roles in getting me on the right track, the blessed journey. The job as a purchasing agent uniquely prepared me to be a

Realtor and business owner. I traded agent roles; I went from being a purchasing agent to being a real estate agent!

The life experiences we have can be used to bring us along the fantastic journey God has for us. There is nothing more important than being where you are supposed to be. Following your dreams and passions are the impetus behind it all.

Fulfillment

I sometimes have to pinch myself to see if this is real. I dreamed of having my own real estate brokerage for years, and know that following my God-given passions led me to where I am now. I'm amazed at how fulfilling each day can be, and how exciting it still is at my age (sixty-one candles at this writing)! The beauty is the innumerable ways we can minister to others when we are flowing in our gifts. We must continually watch for opportunities to be a blessing to others. Because your unique gifts may seem easy and natural, you may be tempted to take them for granted. I have discovered that those talents we have are precious, and can be dispensed to aid and assist others. Truly, this is what God intended. In other words, we need to unwrap our talents or gifts to reveal our calling.

The Journey

The journey to owning my own company was an exciting, thrilling, yet sometimes difficult time, and now that I'm here, where do I go next? A wonderful aspect of God's plan for us is that we never finish the entire journey until He calls us home to heaven. What does that mean to me? That as we walk towards our destiny showing love for others, we grow. As we grow, we learn. As we learn, we have more to give to others. The true meaning of pursuing and fulfilling our passions is to have plenty, barns overflowing. This isn't so we can consume it all on ourselves, but rather that we can help others in any stage of our life. The beautiful aspect of an abundant life is the ability to pass on blessings to others. This encompasses not only financial blessings but wisdom, counsel, friendship, help, and a host of others.

At one time I thought that following my passions meant reaching a destination. In other words, there would be an end, but I have found that following your passions to fulfill your calling and purpose is not a destination. It is a life-long journey, and God changes and adds to it as you follow the path.

My sixtieth birthday turned out to be one of my best. I went down memory lane and decided not to have regrets. At any age, I know I have an amazing life left to pursue. It may be filled with lots of twists, turns, and bounces, but the rest of my life will be the best as long as I'm pursuing my calling and purpose. You know the same goes for you. Now how exciting is that?

Alignment—Your Calling is Sure

I'm thinking about you right now. Yes, you my reader. You were created by a masterful, unlimited, full-of-creativity, and loving God who desires only the best for you! How could you do anything but succeed with this amazing King of Kings and Lord of Lords on your side? Scripture says you were *"fearfully and wonderfully made"* (Psalm 139:14, NIV), and that *"We are His workmanship, created in Christ Jesus for good works"* (Ephesians 2:10, KJV).

Below is an exercise to help get your creative juices flowing. Make sure to work on it when you have some quiet time by yourself, to reflect. You will be amazed at what you come up with.

Your Exercise:

Take a blank piece of lined or unlined paper, and draw two lines down the middle, equally spaced on the page. Now you have three columns. Write at the top of the first column *"Things that excite and make me happy."* Write at the top of the second column *"Things that make me indignant, sad, or angry."* Write at the top of the third column *"Ways I can channel these passions."*

Next, write under each column events or things that occur to you that greatly affect you; things that you feel passionate about "deep down." Be honest with yourself. This is about what you actually feel, not about how you think you should feel. Some examples may be: music and instruments make my life whole, helping those less fortunate is constantly on my mind, or I can't stand hearing about _____.

Read your list when you are done. Tweak it as needed. Number your items from one to ten, ten being the most important to you. You can have duplicate numbers on items if you prefer to.

Finally, prayerfully consider what you have written and ask the Lord for direction on ways to fulfill your passion and purpose. Ask Him to reveal your calling in this. You may have already known but have not been sure about how to proceed. Remember, God is on your side! Baby steps may be the way to start; sometimes volunteering for an activity can help you see more clearly which direction to take. I believe in seeking Godly counsel before making any big life changes.

Here's to a life of blessings and fulfillment as you pursue your God-given calling!

About Virginia Kettler

Virginia "Ginjie" Kettler is the daughter of a career Air Force officer. Born in Washington, D.C., she lived in many places, including Bermuda and Japan. She treasures family and friendships, keeping in touch with childhood friends.

Always active in her community, Virginia is past-president or board member of many organizations: the BCS Association of Realtors, Better Business Bureau, Dispute Resolution Center, Consumer Education Foundation, Small Business Development Center, Brazos Valley Public Purchasing Association, National Purchasing Institute, Texas Purchasing Management Association, Brazos County Appraisal District, and ABWA.

Virginia has excelled in her chosen fields, winning numerous awards including the ABWA's "Woman of the Year," Lifetime Certified Purchasing Manager certification, The Eagle's "Reader's Choice Realtor of the Year," and others.

Virginia graduated from Texas A&M University with a Bachelor of Business Administration in 1977 (management) and earned a Master of Science degree in 1999 (educational human resource development, and distance learning).

Virginia owns her own real estate brokerage in College Station, Texas. She enjoys relaxing with her two dachshunds and loves being involved in her church activities. Traveling and experiencing new places with her friends and family is one of her real pleasures.

Website: *VirginiaKettler.com*

Chapter 5

Authentic Purpose

> "Everything is attainable if you truly believe in yourself and conquer those internal fears that often cause you to question your abilities."
>
> — Anthony McCauley

Authentic Purpose

Anthony McCauley

Each day we make decisions, and whether those decisions are responsible or irresponsible decisions, we make them. Sooner or later in our individual lives we have to talk to ourselves about the reflection that we see in the mirror. We have to debate the voice that fights with us at night that questions our mere existence. More often than not, we walk around in a cloud of comparison and "measuring up" to others because of this self-conscious, sometimes greedy socio-economic world that often pushes vain beauty and material gain.

During this period of self-talk, the questions arise:

"What is my authentic purpose?"

"What is my earthly mission and plan for existing?"

"What needs to be changed so that I can become all that I can be?"

"How will I accomplish my purpose for living once identified?"

As we journey this road to living a true, authentic life, I would like to add a major question—the response of which can either make you or break you—and that questions is, "*Who cares?*" Do *you* even care about the poor decisions you've made in life? Not to diminish the value of family and friends who are affected, but we must first and foremost be true to ourselves. Begin this discovery of splendor for *you*; because *you* want to!

Put Yourself On Top Of the List

Defining who you are from a standpoint of authenticity can be extremely difficult. Many think our authentic purposes are based on what our parents taught us and told us repeatedly about living successful lives. Keeping a list of people who actually care about our success is difficult and often disheartening. It is a sad state of living when you take inventory of relatives and friends, to find only a few who sincerely care about your well-being, accomplishments, and general welfare. Then there are some people who do not have parents, relatives, or children to live for, who live lonely lives with contentment, and still question "who" they are and "why" they exist.

As you complete this entire compilation of stories and life experiences, I challenge you to put yourself on the top of your list. Adjust your internal value meter; care for yourself. I feel everything is attainable if you truly believe in yourself and conquer those internal fears that often cause you to question your abilities.

Document Your Journey:

Keep in touch with your real and true feelings, reasons, and excuses about the fears you face by writing them down.

Your splendor may not be the same as another's splendor. Ask yourself these questions:

> *"Can I take legitimate responsibility and make the right decisions (daily) to overcome the challenges that hinder my progression?"*

> *"Can I admit that I need help, find the tools, and get the training needed to identify my authentic purpose and mission?"*

My Journey to Self-Discovery

My process of discovery started with *me*! I had to answer these questions, and face these same fears that stifled my abilities. To be transparent, I still fight with some internal fears; some days are better than others. I have endured many setbacks, and this process of living victoriously is a daily commitment. Millions of times I over-rationalize my situation and outcome before making a decision. Ultimately, this was only a way of creating excuses that left me distant from what I knew as my own truth of existence.

My struggles came from a history of chemical dependency which led to an addictive behavior lifestyle that was fruitless, vain, pointless, and without purpose. In the midst of this ruthless ride of addiction, I often ignored the voice of hope telling me that I have an authentic purpose for being on this earth. I gave up on believing that life was worth living! Inside my mind I had brief periods of clarity that would allow me to continue working towards those dreams that had been shown to me from an early age.

Document Your Journey:

Get still and reflect on your moments of clarity. Where were you? What did you hear?

In high school, I thought becoming a professional athlete was going to be the plan for my life. At an early age I would excel in all three sports I played, always with a competitive winning attitude! No one ever told me injury was a reality when you sacrifice your body playing sports. As a result of injury, my professional athletic career goals were eliminated early. I lost sight of life beyond the scoreboard and fans in high school.

After years of cocaine and alcohol abuse, I began to dwindle away from where God was taking me. Authentic purpose and mission cannot be a reality when you have a lot of junk going on inside of your mind, body, and soul.

Authentic purpose and mission has nothing to do with your socio-economic status. Over the years, I have heard others brag about where they were from and what they had accomplished in the past, with expectations that their inheritance or title would exempt them or win them favors. Being raised in a small town I didn't have the same chances of title and wealthy inheritance, but I had a way of scheming and manipulating my way through life with my smile and personality. Again this was an epic fail on my part! The art of scheming and manipulation left a trail of hurt for those close to me, and it definitely left me drifting away from authentic purpose and mission. I was convinced that my setbacks were too appalling for me to recover from them, so I compromised and repeated the same cycle of drug abuse and drinking. Bad habits will lead you to interfering with your life's purposes. You will begin to question if you are on the right path, and you will begin to question if you are making right decisions. I found myself dancing and flirting with an unguided existence that led to a rock bottom!

My purpose and your purpose for being here on earth is different. Just like no two fingerprints will match one another, we may face similar trials but every person must have a unique and individual realization of their purpose in life.

I will share with you some of the ways I dealt with my setbacks that have gotten me to this point of complete surrender and faith—which has become strength to me. My life was predestined, and there was nothing I could do about it except continue to enhance what God has put inside of me. I had to deal with seeking to know the truth about my authentic self. The first thing I had to do was admit I have no power over chemical dependency.

Discover the Diamonds on Your Journey:

Write a statement about what you believe in. This may be a faith based statement that includes positive statements or affirmations that help you overcome negative thoughts and defeating self-talk.

    Authentic purpose and authentic mission must involve a commitment and acceptance that we do not merely exist. The deeply entrenched negative thinking had me walking in a desert looking for a drink machine. Yes . . . I was disillusioned!

    Disillusionment will keep you from your authentic purpose and mission; instead of focusing on your spiritual direction, your motivation will become clouded with despair, and your foundation will feel like quicksand, with nothing to stand on. You'll question everything. As you read these words, you may be in awe wondering, *"Can I truly find this authentic purpose and mission for myself?"* The answer is, *"Yes"*!

    Let's answer the last question about dealing with the proper resources, and accepting help to become the best you can be in life. You may have noticed my reference of belief in a higher power, of which I choose to call God. I am a Christ follower first and foremost! Identify your faith; whatever that might be. This is important to discovering your authenticity. My faith in God has allowed me to adjust my self-talk, seek truth, and walk in my purpose and mission. I spend time in prayer, meditation, and fasting. This cultivates my mental and emotional basis of maintaining the authentic purpose and mission for my life.

I repeat this to myself and I know that God speaks to me, and shows me how to work things out; He constantly reveals the purpose for my life. As I stay focused on knowing that God will take care of me, I change my mindset to focus on the decisions that enhance my life. Guess what? I inventory anything that doesn't add to my level of faith and confidence. If I am around people or in a situation that rehearses or breeds negativity in my emotions, it needs to be removed. Then and only then, can I continue to walk in the true power of unleashing my purpose and mission.

At this present moment in my life, the things that I walked away from thirty years ago are coming full circle.

Discover the Diamonds on Your Journey:

Make a list of people in your life. Give each person a plus sign (+) or a minus sign (-) to show if they are adding or subtracting to the positive emotions and decisions in your life.

During times of active addiction I constantly expected better days to come (even when it may not have looked that bad on the outside). I had a deep sense of expectancy. Rearranging my life, and the people around me, was the first step of restoration to complete faithfulness. This helped me to realize that better days were in store for me. This journey of unleashing the power and authentic purpose for my life had to become a broadening of my horizons—beyond what I like to call "stinking-thinking," and beyond a selfish attitude regarding chemical dependency and alcoholism.

I truly wanted to know what my purpose was for living! Enough is enough! My body was shutting down due to the abuse. My thinking was not focused on a bright future, and I had no dominion and power over cocaine and alcohol. I had to get to the point of no longer considering my life as my own. There had to become a humbling within my soul. Learning humility was critical for me to walk humbly with my God, and it was necessary so that I could remove the resentments of not being a musician (one of my high school desires before football). I also had to deal with the resentments of not following through on my dreams of entrepreneurship. Humility helped me to have an attitude of gratitude for God's spirit within me!

I had to arise from the ashes of addiction some kind of way! I had to keep the self-talk going louder than the insanity of my actions, some of which left me controlled by each and every situation. This didn't provide me with a balanced perspective to line up with unleashing my purpose and mission for my life.

The self-centeredness and all of those selfish desires that I harbored where roadblocks that left me blind to discovering my splendor! Overcoming *myself* was my gift to *me*! I was able to choose a path of diligently seeking out "good" for my life.

Today, I work continuously both on gaining resources and working the tools to maintain my authentic purpose and mission. This involves working with other individuals whose lives are affected by drugs and alcohol. This is my duty: to reach back and bring a message of hope with motivation and encouragement to people, and to be a light in a dark world!

I am to provide support from a genuine standpoint of telling my life story that will plant seeds of hope in those who have lost all hope for existence.

In addition to *documenting your journey* and *discovering your diamonds* along the way, here are a few suggestions that will help you discover your splendor and unleash anything that hinders your life. Keep in mind that this is not a one-time fix, but a daily lifestyle of maintenance and commitment that has to be refreshed often as you get older and as situations change in your life. Don't die in the process, and don't quit! Believe in the process and work it to the best of your ability.

1. The *removal* process: this will take some time and great sacrifice. *Remove* any thing or any person that is not enhancing your life if it results in physical, mental, emotional pain. If you have no power over it, *remove* it!

2. The *expectation* process: this can be a tough part of self-talk. *Expect* your life to be different from day to day. What do you want? Obtain a sense of *expectancy* that you will find your authentic purpose and mission for being on earth.

3. The *prayer & meditation* process: these two parts incorporated together—daily and consistently—will guide you into truth and help you unleash the junk that keeps you away from purpose and mission. Warning: you will not feel like *praying and meditating* each day. Some days will be easier than others.

4. The *belief* process: once you identify your faith-based foundation, you must take ownership of the precepts and inner guidance tools that reaffirm your divine purpose. When situations make you question yourself, and when your self-talk becomes negative, it is your *belief* that will keep you nailed down to your authentic purpose and mission, which is *yours* to walk in while you are here on earth!

Anthony McCauley

About Anthony McCauley

Anthony B. McCauley knows all too well how tough it is to discover your splendor and live an authentic life consistently... with a made-up mind!

A native of Thomasville, North Carolina, Anthony has dealt with his own personal struggles pertaining to chemical dependency and alcoholism since high school. He's an outreach minister and national speaker with a message of experience, strength, and hope for those who've lost hope on the lifelong journey to recovery. Anthony lives by his philosophy, *"In order to keep what I have, I must freely give it away."*

His early work includes vocational training as a Drug and Alcohol Treatment Specialist, with current work in a Florida-based behavioral health treatment center.

Currently Anthony is pursuing his psychology degree at Southern New Hampshire University (Manchester, New Hampshire) with a concentration in Addiction Counseling, and a goal to complete Doctoral studies in this field. October 2015, he was inducted into The National Society of Leadership and Success (Sigma Alpha Pi), an invitation only leadership organization for students who consistently maintain above average GPA. He currently resides in Jacksonville, Florida. He boasts as a proud graduate with academic and tri-athletic honors from Thomasville High School, where his parents Bernard and Mary McCauley still reside. Make no mistake, Anthony is a *Hope Dealer!*

Website: *SetBackForTheComeBack.com*

Chapter 6

It's Okay

"Only you—and you alone—can change your life for the better; and only you—and you alone—will know your true life's calling or mission."

Heather McKim

It's O.K.

Heather McKim

When I was asked to be a part of this book, I was flattered and terrified. Life Purpose? Calling in life? My mission?

Perhaps in my mid-forties I am to know what these things are, but I have to be honest, I don't.

Just when I think I've figured out what my life mission or purpose in life is, it changes. No matter how sure I am that this is "it," inevitably it isn't. So here I sit trying to tell you what my life purpose or mission in life is . . . and I'm stumped.

For me and people like me, committing yourself to one life purpose or mission is daunting. I have spent much of my life taking five steps forward and four steps back. I have never, no matter how hard I've tried, been able to fit myself into any mold. I've always just been me. So in deciding how to start this project I first considered writing about how my life's purpose was to be unapologetically myself, including the ugly and the crazy. Maybe it is in a way. I find it very hard to change who I am, and I feel as though compromising myself for the sake of another is one of the worst things I could do.

In many stages of my life, I thought I had it all figured out; but just as soon as I figured it out it changed. I once thought my life mission was to be a great wife and mother. I've tried the wife thing . . . twice. It doesn't seem to be my thing. So then, am I here to be the world's greatest mother? Doubtful. I mean I love my children and I brought them into the world; their life purpose is their own and I'd like to think that once the mothering is over (if it ever really is), I've still got some significant value.

Maybe It's the Sibling Connection

When I was younger I hung my hat on the fact that I'm the eldest child. There's a lot of research on the effects of siblings, and how the order of our birth affects the way we shape our behaviors. I was the eldest, until I met the older brother I did not realize I had, and then that theory was kind of thrown out the window. Sure, I still acted as the oldest for most of my life, but it threw a wrench into the explanation of me.

After I found out I was no longer the eldest, my younger (but not youngest) brother died of cancer. For many years growing up it was just him and me. I fully believed that I was one thing because he was another. For instance, I was really good at writing, spelling and English whereas he was really good at math and sports (he was also my mother's favorite but I'll save that for a different book). I naively thought that he would long outlive me and so the idea of who I was then was a pretty sound one. Then he died and I had to reinvent myself in a way; who was I if he was not here?

It is a strange thing, that sibling connection. Lucky for me I'm close with all of my siblings; these are relationships I will never take for granted.

Maybe It's a Relationship

In my first marriage I was pretty sure I had my life all figured out, despite the fact I was in my early twenties. I had a growing career, married someone who had money, owned my own home outright, and I had a gorgeous baby boy. To the outside world I was a pretty lucky girl. Inside though, I may have been the unhappiest girl on the planet.

When I became single (for the first time), I will be honest, I was lost. I had no clue about life purpose or mission; it didn't even hit my radar. I did however, date a lot of men and I'll tell you what, it was not what I expected. Dating many men over the course of the next few years just made me feel lonelier than ever. I could not believe there were so many people out there but none that "got" me. None that made me tick.

In my second marriage, I felt that despite the differences between us, he and I could make it work. Ignoring some warning signs and advice of some friends, I dove into this marriage full force. I was now a mother and step-mother. Still, I had no idea what I was passionate about. I had no idea what I wanted out of life. Like most people, all I ever really wanted was to be happy, and as narcissistic as this may sound, I really wanted to find someone who just loved me, all of me. Needless to say, things did not work out as planned.

Tapping Into Something New

In the fall of 2013 I was laid off from a job at which I was very skilled. However, I was not feeling passionate about my contribution to the world at the time and decided that applying to the police force was something I really wanted to do. I mention this simply because I want you to know that in life, there are many sides of ourselves we never tap into. We never tap into them because we are afraid. No one expected that I wanted to be a cop and only the closest people to me went *"Aha! That makes perfect sense."* Most others were shocked but wished me well as I started my journey. I did this for one year. I trained and I pushed myself. It is important for you to know that I changed my entire way of thinking during this time; I had to. I separated myself from the politically correct business person I had become. I donated my suits to charity and threw my politically correct and professional ways out the window. I'm the type of woman who dives into everything one hundred percent; this includes marriage, jobs, and mothering. Without going into full details, I enjoyed every second that I spent training with the police and I met so many amazing women. Once again I thought for sure I had found my life's mission and purpose, and once again I was wrong.

What I Know for Certain; It's Okay

So here I am, a forty something single mother (of two now) and a blogger who has been asked to write a chapter in a book about life purpose, calling, and mission, and I have no idea what to tell you. Yes, there are a couple of things I do know *for sure* (sorry Oprah)!

It is *okay* to not know what your calling or mission is in life. Seriously. Stop running around in a crazy frenzy trying to figure it out. Someday, it will hit you. Stop thinking about it, and enjoy your life.

I am an amazing person. Yes, all of this despite two failed marriages. I know that I am a good and loving person. I know that I will take care of those I love and that I will always give my last penny to a starving stranger. Also, an amazing thing happens when you turn forty. You start to appreciate yourself! Yes, maybe I'm "nuts" sometimes. Maybe I'm over-emotional or too loud. Maybe I have too many opinions or perhaps I'm too opinionated. It's ok. It's who I am.

I have taken everything that's been thrown at me in my life, and I've survived it. Let's call this quantum biology. I have survived the death of a parent and a sibling, and the failure of a dream. I have survived being cheated on and downsized, and I've survived divorce and despair, and all of these things make me *exactly* who I am today.

Trust

In spite of having always been an impatient person, I decided to "*trust life a little bit.*" This comes straight out of the mouth of Maya Angelou, who seemed to have her life figured out.

I need to trust that I will know in due time what my mission and calling is in life, and that one of the most important things I can do in the meantime is not compromise who I am as a person. I am here for a reason. I am here to make a difference. I do not yet know how or when but I will. As I mentioned earlier, five steps forward and four steps back.

I encourage you to think of the almighty arrow. If it is not pulled back it doesn't gain momentum. The further back it is pulled the more momentum it gains. Sometimes no matter how tough it is, we need to go backwards before moving forward.

In your own life journey, don't let the negativity of others drag you down. Don't change who you are at the core of your person; embrace it. Not everyone is going to love you. Heck, not everyone is even going to like you despite your best efforts.

It's Okay

It's Okay to fail and it is okay to fail more than once. It's okay to do things of which others do not approve; if you feel you need to do them for yourself, then do them. If you've spent your entire life to this point making every single decision as a direct reflection of how others might think of you, or if you've made the majority of your decisions based in fear, stop now. Start living the life you want. In the end what is going to matter is that you were kind and that you tried your best.

Take risks and take chances. If you are too comfortable, move. If you are unhappy, change it. If you feel you can do better, then do so. Only you—and you alone—can change your life for the better; and only you—and you alone—will know your true life's calling or mission.

About Heather McKim

Heather is a business professional, successful blogger, and single mother of two who thoroughly enjoys running and hiking, and is always ready for any adventure. In her spare time, she enjoys writing, reading, cooking, and connecting with her family. Heather is a woman who loves finding inspiration in the little things in life.

She's a captivating writer who is well-known for being direct, down to earth, and to the point. Her popular blog, *The Back 40*, is all about matters of the heart and Heather's thoughts and experiences on life after forty that are often common to us all. She shares on topics relating to love, relationships, growing up without a father, and life in general.

Website: *The-Back40.blogspot.com*

Chapter 7

Laughing at the Future

"Long-term purpose guides your direction; short-term goals keep the dream alive."

Karen VanMatre Smith

Laughing at the Future

Karen V. Smith

" . . . *She can laugh at the days to come.*"

Proverbs 31:25 (NIV)

Dreams are funny things. Sometimes, it seems the bigger your dream, the further away it is and the more discouraged you feel. Yet, without long-term dreams, goals, and vision, life feels empty, and we can feel less and less important . . . less significant. So, how does a person balance inspiring vision with the mundane here-and-now? That's what this chapter is about.

Zig Ziglar once said, "*If you shoot for nothing, you'll hit it every time.*" How true. It was true for me. As young woman, I had given up my own education to raise a large family. Now, my kids are great—don't misunderstand, and the privilege of having ten years at home to influence them and start them off right is something I treasure . . . in retrospect. At the time, though, it was mundane. Oh, the kids themselves were anything but mundane, but daily life as a homemaker made me feel further and further from my big dream.

You see, at seven years old I had an epiphany. I believe it came from above, for me. I was to be a doctor, and not just any doctor, but a missionary doctor. Maybe it was because I really felt I should also be a public speaker, and in the tradition in which I was raised, girls just couldn't do that . . . unless they were missionaries.

So, here I was, with a home full of small, exuberant children. Diapers. Home-schooling. Dishes. Laundry. Isolation. And a big vision, tailor-made for me, that seemed further and further away. Depression set in. Hopelessness. Loneliness. Worthlessness . . . and guilt, for even wanting more. Then one day, while washing dishes in my country kitchen, it hit me. I could live my dream and still love my family. Or I could spend the rest of my life wondering, *"What if?"*

I was thirty.

Taking a shot was scary. Any risk I took now involved seven people, not just me, but I took it; and my precious husband and five amazing kids decided, after a few bobbles, to take the shot with me. It would take me four years to get there, but . . . I did! It really happened. I was accepted at one of the top ten medical/scientific institutions in the world. Really. From dirty dishes to freshman classes taught by Nobel laureates, and we made it through, together.

I have now been a physician for a decade. I am also a licensed minister with regular speaking engagements. I love my life. My children are grown, stable, and happy, and I am becoming a regular on short-term mission ventures. Many of them involve training young doctors; raising my family was invaluable preparation. Getting into medical school took planning and preparation, over a number of years. That's okay. If you don't start, you'll never arrive, and you can enjoy the journey, no matter your particular big dream. I'd like to share some principles that helped me along the way.

Deliberate Joy

During a rough time in ancient Israel, one leader made a difference. The people had lost sight of their identity and purpose, and not lived up to their heaven-sent identities and goals. Their ruler had this to say, as they wept: *"Do not grieve, for the joy of the Lord is your strength"* (Nehemiah 8:10b, NIV).

That's a tough call when you feel like you've messed up, fallen short, or not stepped up to be who you know you are, but it is the only way out.

There was one major obstacle I had to overcome, after that kitchen-window epiphany, to begin reaching for my dreams. It was huge, and at times, insurmountable. What was it? Ah, that's simple. My biggest obstacle was . . . me.

I found myself plagued by a deep depression, and I might be able to blame it on bearing five children in a seven-year period. It is true, that may have contributed, chemically, but there was a bigger component: my thinking. I had developed so many negative thoughts that I was afraid to move, and definitely ashamed to be myself. Now, no one knew I thought that way. On the surface I was a smiling, busy, well-liked young mother, but below the serene, rippling surface were deadly rocks. The combination of fear and shame is crippling. Yet the antidote was so simple. Joy.

So many people are waiting on happiness. They reason that when they achieve their big dreams and goals, they will have reason to celebrate. It doesn't work that way. It takes positive, forward motion to get there, and the fuel for the engine that moves you forward is . . . joy. Not happiness. What's the difference? Joy is deliberate. You do it on purpose. Happiness is a reaction; joy is a response.

Pardon me while I slip into my doctor voice for a second. You see, your brain is made up of organized cells, floating in a sea of chemicals. Those chemicals can, of course, make you feel happy or sad, angry or depressed, or even euphoric or in love. Western society has become aware of this. It's what Prozac is all about. The movie *Inside Out* also touched on this idea.

But the reverse is also true (and this is, frankly, where the movie missed it). When someone chooses a positive thought, it changes the expression of the different chemicals in the brain. It's an amazing medical paradox: while neurotransmitters (brain chemicals) can affect our moods and our decisions, our moods, thoughts, and decisions can also have an effect on which brain chemicals are produced.

If one of us simply accepts a down or depressed thought, negative emotions and chemistries are generated. They then create more down emotions and depressed thoughts, which create more negative chemistry. A downward spiral develops.

If left unchallenged, this thought/emotion/chemistry interaction can trap a person for life.

Modern western science, with its focus on God-less fact, has unintentionally left us feeling helpless regarding sadness, despair, and depression. Having heard of the role of our brain chemistry, we feel powerless to affect change, but . . . there's another side to the story.

Eastern medicine, a more spiritual way exemplified by practices like Ayurveda and yoga, have long held that the mind can be trained, affecting the body. God is neither Eastern nor Western; both practices fall short of His wisdom. Dr. Henry Emmons is an integrative psychiatrist from Northfield, Minnesota. He integrates, or puts together, Western medicine and Eastern thought. In his wonderful book, *The Chemistry of Joy*, Dr. Emmons lays out ideas for dealing with negative thoughts and emotions in the arena of the mind, and not just in the physical brain. Faith helps. To believe in something so crazy that it could only come true if God steps in is an exhilarating adventure. Forgiveness is a huge part of healing. And purposeful generosity has a place.

You can create an upward spiral.

For me, I gathered wisdom. I read great books on mental health and creating your own future. I prayed for wisdom, and received it from unexpected avenues. Church was one place I received wisdom and healing, and it helped tremendously, but so did psychologists and professors and great books I encountered in the grocery store.

Step-by-step, I walked out of the darkness. Thankfully so; my life was at risk during part of the process. And, in fifteen years I have never walked back.

Joy is about many things: gratitude, courage, boundaries, identity, patience, and peace. But, for me, at its root it is about faith. Alcoholics Anonymous is famous for helping people out of addiction by teaching them to depend on a higher power. My God was too small for my goals; but I had made Him that way. And my conception of God was like a straitjacket, keeping me from living my life. When I opened up my heart, I found He was bigger than I could ever have imagined. And there was room in Him for me—just the way He had created me. It's time to take the limits off.

Like Abraham in the Bible, God is saying to you, "*Lift up your eyes.*" He has given you a magnificent place. You may not be designed to be a missionary doctor; probably you aren't. We're a little weird. You are designed, however, to be a magnificent you, unlimited and courageous. There is a specific goal for your life: walking out your God-designed place at a level you can't even imagine right now. Joy is, quite simply, the fuel for the fire.

Persistent Preparation

Another key to success in any area is . . . getting ready.

When my youngest daughter was a young girl, she was involved in a ballet company. We found that she did better after hours and hours of practice and rehearsal. As a dance mom, I found I could help her by showing up early, with bobby pins, makeup, sewing kits, and food. I had my own "preparations" to make before every large performance.

What separates a daydream or a fantasy from a goal is . . . action. The Chinese philosopher Laozi (604 BC-531 BC), a contemporary of Confucius, famously said, *"The journey of a thousand miles begins with a single step."*

It is fundamental. If you really believe you will get there, you will begin. If you don't take small steps, one of two things is happening: either you don't really want to go, or you're afraid you may fail.

Our foundational thought *"She can laugh at the days to come,"* is the second part of a two-part sentence. The entire thought reads, *"She is clothed with strength and dignity; she can laugh at the days to come"* (Proverbs 31:25, NIV). This is in conclusion to a longer chapter. Throughout this famous chapter, this person spent a tremendous amount of time on one thing: preparation. Set in an ancient culture, it details spinning, weaving, trading in the marketplace, and managing a large affluent home. Every action described is the action of someone preparing for the future. Whether it involves clothing, food, the home environment, or investing wisdom and conversation in others, she is always making deposits for the future.

The reason our proverbial homemaker could laugh at the future was because she had spent so much effort preparing for it. She was unlikely to be caught unaware, and very likely to reach her goals.

Malcolm Gladwell wrote an interesting book, called *The Tipping Point*. Using the lives of well-known and successful people, he points out what it took to get them there. He found that, on the whole, successful people spent about ten thousand hours practicing their crafts before becoming influential. The average work-year is calculated at roughly two thousand hours in America (forty hours a week for fifty weeks, with two weeks of vacation per year). That means that with a full-time commitment to improve in an area, it would take at least five years to reach critical mass.

An all-time favorite person of mine is a famous preacher's wife named Gloria Copeland. She is known for her spunky, honest, and simple approach to life, using the Bible. I heard her say once, *"What if God called you to be a doctor? You say, 'Gloria, I can't do that. It would take ten years.' Well, where will be you in ten years if you don't do it? Ten years older and still not a doctor."*

Most of us will spend a number of years on this earth. How we invest those years determines our return. What would you do if you knew that you could be successful within five years? What goals would you reach for? How would you do it?

My steps toward transitioning from college drop-out and homemaker to award-winning physician were simple; step one, I finished college . . . check that box. How? I got on AmericaOnline (many years ago now) and asked for help from an online educational counselor. She found me a program I was close to completing already. I did that. Then I went to graduate school and improved my GPA by working hard in my classes for two more years. I went to seminars on how to interview for medical school. I researched the necessary coursework to be considered. I took a course to prepare for the MCAT (Medical College Admission Test). I set my course by my bigger vision, but became faithful in the daily details and minutiae involved in each step along the way. I did all of this while juggling peanut butter sandwiches, refereeing arguments, and helping with the PTA.

There was more. I was concerned about my two youngest daughters; they had never gone to daycare. We put them in a part-time preschool to get them used to the idea. I delayed my medical school entrance until it was right for them, too. I built bonds with my older children. We started one-on-one "date nights" so that no one felt lost in the crowd. When my husband had a job change involving a choice of two different locations, we chose the one with two medical schools in town. I was accepted at one of them.

If you are a singer, you may need to begin rehearsals and book studio time. Maybe this year all that is available to do is sing around the house while you do other things. Start there; watch for opportunities to open. You'll be ready when they come. If you're a musician, set aside daily practice time. If your dream is art, take a class at the community college. If you're into musical theatre, join the local troupe. You may have to earn your stripes building sets and having one-line roles before you're ready for a lead. Do it. You won't get there if you don't start.

One of my favorite people is an acting and vocal coach who teaches young people in our community. He is famous for saying, *"Do the work of an actor."* He expects them to research the role, the play, and the playwright. He expects them to dive deep into the emotions the character may feel, and portray them. If they are in a musical, he expects ninety minutes daily of vocal practice. I have never heard him mention "talent." He always references "work." In an industry full of talented people, he has learned that he can count on the ones who show up and invest the time in preparation.

A final thought on preparation . . . what if, during creation, God had dropped Adam in on day four? He would have been bobbing in the ocean with nothing to eat. Timing is everything. People like to say *"The devil's in the details."* While that can be true, what is truer is that the small things are very important to God. He is absolutely in the details. And He can get you from here to there, if you take consistent, small steps with excellence.

During the years I was in medical school, we lived in a simple three bedroom home (with the garage redone as a suite for the boys), in a middle-class community. I would frequently jog two miles around the community. Unfortunately, to get home, I had to spend the last half-mile running up a gently sloping hill. It was tough for me at the time. I learned to put my head down and look at the sidewalk while I ran. I would give myself kudos as each large square of sidewalk disappeared beneath my feet. Eventually I would look up and be at the top of the hill. It became a great metaphor for my education. As a third year medical student, I had to report for duty at four in the morning to draw blood and take vital signs—in addition to diagnosing and treating patients—only to be harshly critiqued by a supervising physician no matter what I did. So I thought of each day as a block in that sidewalk, and I made it to the top.

Expansive Vision

I never would have made it, if at the bottom of the hill I hadn't looked at the top and committed to get there. Long-term purpose guides your direction; short-term goals keep the dream alive.

Oral Roberts is an interesting man. He built a full university on land that was a pasture in the 1940s, when he began. Today its graduates number in the thousands and have affected lives all over the world, in every area of society. His oft-repeated motto, posted around campus, is paraphrased from Johann Wolfgang von Goethe, and reads, *"Make no small plans here."* (Goethe's original quote is, *"Dream no small dreams for they have no power to move the hearts of men."*)

When I went back to school to prepare to apply to medical school, I had to retake physics, and I found out something interesting. We measure things like cars, trains, airplanes, and bullets with something called vectors.

A vector is like a line segment, except that it has direction and speed. So, if a train is going to go thirty miles per hour in a northeast direction, you could draw it as a vector. It looks like an arrow, with the tip pointed in the direction in which you are going.

So, I created *Karen's Vector Theory of Life*. It's actually quite simple: direction trumps speed... *every time*! I actually don't care how fast that train is moving, if I need to go from Dallas to Boston and it's headed for Phoenix, direction matters most; and direction requires a big-picture view.

The Bible is full of ordinary folks who accomplished extraordinary things after being given . . . vision. There's David, the family-baby and shepherd boy who would become King; Joseph, the jailbird who would be prime minister of Egypt; Esther, the captive who would become Queen of Babylon after a near-miss as a concubine; and Mary, the (we think) fourteen year-old good girl, whose out-of-wedlock child would change the whole world.

Each of them had to embrace their calling, and begin to step it out. There were obstacles . . . setbacks. But they kept their eyes on the prize, and were each ultimately incredibly successful. That's why we know their names.

Several years ago, I read a biography of a missionary teacher. A single woman, all of her life she had longed to be a missionary. The Great Depression held her back when she was young. At fifty-nine, she was finally accepted. It seemed that the age cutoff at that time was sixty years old. Young-looking and healthy, she would spend twenty years in China teaching and mentoring college students before anyone remembered to check her age. She expressed her disgust and frustration upon being made to return home in her eighties.

My point? It's not too late. Dream that dream. Fulfill that calling. Manage that destiny. Don't just do what you're born to do; finish it. Hit the high note; prepare for the big impact. Jesus did. Paul did, and you, too, can run your race and finish your course. But you have to start.

Big vision requires a couple of things. Oral Roberts, who built that university from nothing which I referenced above, says to do this: 1) Find out what is the will of God, and 2) Confer no more with flesh and blood.

That's preacher-speak for *"Don't listen to the naysayers."* There are amazing people you can confide your dreams to, and they will support and help you. But be picky; not everyone is really your friend when it comes to fulfilling your calling. Jealousy can come from the most unlikely places (read: people who aren't fulfilling their own destinies. If they were, they wouldn't have time to mess with yours.)

Look at the vision until it is bigger in your mind than present reality: bigger than the naysayers, and bigger than your own doubts and fears. And when you hit a rough patch, lift up your eyes and gaze on it again.

In between, set your course and keep your head down. But come up for air, and a big-picture course check, every time you need to.

Play Offense

Deliberate Joy, *Persistent Preparation*, and *Expansive Vision*: these are decisions from which there is no retreat.

These are the tools I used to step into my own purpose and calling. I have never regretted it. Neither has my family. My sons and daughters are empowered individuals who are walking out their own life journeys, partly due to my example—even back then, when I was scared stiff.

You have enemies: doubt, fear, jealous people, small-minded people, people who want you in their lives in order to fulfill *them*. That's okay. You can make it; those things are things we all have to face.

I fully believe that anyone who steps out into their own identity, calling, and purpose stops being jealous of anyone else. Why would you want to be someone else when your own calling and purpose is so marvelous, and . . . so perfect for you?

So do it. Be you, and play offense. Football games are helped by the defense, but they are never won there. Football games are won by a consistent, complex, multifaceted attempt at gaining ground, in spite of the setbacks, obstacles, and naysayers.

A friend once told me that right before you wake up, you dream. So go ahead, dream. And wake up to the you who you were always meant to be.

About Karen V. Smith, MD

Karen V. Smith is dedicated to seeing women reach their potential in God—spirit, soul, and body. Whether in speaking and writing, hanging out with her daughters, volunteering, or in her practice as a medical doctor, healing and helping women is her recurring theme.

Dr. Smith is a family physician, educator, and licensed Christian minister. She holds a Bachelor of Science degree in Liberal Arts, a Master's degree in Education, and was awarded the MD degree by UT Southwestern Medical School, recently named among the top ten science institutions in the world.

She is a fellow of the American Academy of Family Physicians, and has helped train young doctors since 2006. She's been named a "Top Doc" by the medical community of Fort Worth, Texas, for the last three consecutive years and has been active in many volunteer organizations. However, she considers her greatest accomplishments the raising of her five children, the building of a twenty-eight year marriage, and her ministry work in other nations.

Website: *KarenVSmith.wordpress.com*

Conclusion

Do What You Must

"I pray that the eyes of your heart may be enlightened in order that you may know the hope to which he has called you, the riches of his glorious inheritance in his holy people, and his incomparably great power for us who believe."

Ephesians 1:18-19a (NIV)

Do What You Must

Many people mistake humiliation for humility. Should you find the wherewithal to realize the grandest accomplishments in the annals of mankind, it will only bring pleasure to God *if* your goal is to bring honor and glory to Him. So the message from this messenger is that you should: take pride in what you do. When we do our best, it honors God by showing Him we appreciate what He has given us!

The truth is that there are no common men. The estate of manhood is an "in the image of God" proposition. The late Dr. Francis Schaeffer penned the words *"There are no little people. There are no small places."* God means for each of our journeys to be significant and meaningful. Man's saga is meant to be a moving journey full of mystery, marvel, and dynamic adventure.

The work of the great dreamer is often a lonely vigil blessed with hard moments and deep sacrifices. Yet, the art creation must be drawn, whether anyone sees it or not. The literary work must be written, whether the audience finds it in the author's lifetime or not. Such is the compulsion of the artist, author, creator, and dreamer.

If you must create, you must create! It is like the allure of the ocean to a seaman. You must voyage whether or not others sense the call. It calls your name with a moving sense of destiny. You must fulfill it, because it is in you! The dream must come forth. Melville's classic *Moby Dick* didn't achieve commercial success and notoriety until after Melville's death, and so it often is with the dreamer. The call is strong. The mission is moving. The desire is compelling. You must give in to the high call of its celestial chords, to find peace and fulfillment in this life.

My sister Detra was a magnificent artist. I have her inspirations all over my home. Her work still inspires me with awe! She was driven to create works of art and sculpture. She was driven to write. I have four of her novels that I hope to publish, posthumously for her. The Makers mark was on her!

And that's the way it is. The greatest thing you can do, is what you *must* do! It is your divine duty to give vent to the mark of the eternal on your soul. So my message is: sing your song if no one but God listens. Your passionate heartsong is the fingerprint of God. Sing the celestial melody. Give expression to the passion of your soul. Live up to your divine potential and give the glory to God, for your creations.

SLAM (a.k.a. Timothy Grant Carter)

Contact the Coauthors

Timothy Grant Carter
Website: GutsIsTheKey.com

Margo DeGange
Website: MargoDeGange.com

Dorothy-Inez Del Tufo
Website: DorothyInez.com

Virginia Kettler
Website: VirginiaKettler.com

Anthony McCauley
Website: SetBackForTheComeBack.com

Heather McKim
Website: The-Back40.blogspot.com

Karen V. Smith
Website: KarenVSmith.wordpress.com

Splendor Publishing

Splendor Publishing's life-changing books are written by skilled and passionate leaders, entrepreneurs, and experts with a mission to make a positive impact in the lives of others.

Splendor books inspire and encourage personal, professional, and spiritual growth. For information about our book titles, authors, or publishing process, or for wholesale ordering for conferences, seminars, events, or training, visit SplendorPublishing.com.

Notes:

Notes:

Notes:

Notes:

www.ingramcontent.com/pod-product-compliance
Lightning Source LLC
LaVergne TN
LVHW051841080426
835512LV00018B/2999